Speech, Language and Communication for Healthy Little Minds

This book is packed with practical ideas and techniques to enable early years educators to support the communication development of the children in their setting and to understand the relationship between communication and emotional wellbeing.

By forming an understanding of the science behind emotional regulation and the role of the adult in supporting the development of this, the book explores how emotions can impact learning and communication skills, and why we must understand how adult responses and communication have a direct impact on emotional wellbeing.

Each chapter provides:

- practical ideas which will create a culture of communication and connection;
- research and case studies with plenty of opportunities for the reader to reflect on their own practice and interaction style;
- top tips and ideas for promoting speech and language skills in the early years environment; and
- an awareness of how to support the language development and emotional wellbeing of children who are struggling to communicate.

Emotions impact interactions, and interactions impact communication and connectedness. This book enables and empowers the reader to understand what communication and wellbeing really look like in the early years environment, and how we can use this knowledge to improve long-term outcomes for children's learning and mental health. It is essential reading for all early years educators.

Becky Poulter Jewson has over 25 years of experience working with children and families as a qualified early years lead and is the director of early years and author for Thriving Language Community Interest Company. She has led and developed teams of successful early years educators within children's centres and the private sector. Having owned her own nursery and pre-school, Becky has developed free-flow provision and language-rich learning environments throughout the country. Becky believes that empowering individuals to thrive and helping to create future generations is probably the best career in the world! She is a passionate advocate for early years and supports many further teaching and learning facilities.

Rebecca Skinner qualified as a speech and language therapist in 2001 and is the director of speech and language therapy and author for Thriving Language Community Interest Company. Alongside her work at Thriving Language, Rebecca works as a speech and language therapist for the NHS, specialising in early years and cleft palate. She is passionate about communication and interaction, and the role that the adult plays in the development of this. Rebecca believes that being able to communicate is a basic human right and we must respect all ways of communicating.

Little Minds Matter:

Promoting Social and Emotional Wellbeing in the Early Years

Series Adviser: Sonia Mainstone-Cotton

The *Little Minds Matter* series promotes best practice for integrating social and emotional health and wellbeing into the early years setting. It introduces practitioners to a wealth of activities and resources to support them in each key area: providing access to ideas for unstructured, imaginative outdoor play; activities to create a sense of belonging and form positive identities; and, importantly, strategies to encourage early years professionals to create a workplace that positively contributes to their own wellbeing, as well as the quality of their provision. The *Little Minds Matter* series ensures that practitioners have the tools they need to support every child.

A Guide to Mental Health for Early Years Educators
Putting Wellbeing at the Heart of Your Philosophy and Practice
Kate Moxley

Supporting the Wellbeing of Children with EAL
Essential Ideas for Practice and Reflection
Liam Murphy

Building Positive Relationships in the Early Years
Conversations to Empower Children, Professionals, Families and Communities
Sonia Mainstone-Cotton and Jamel Carly Campbell

Developing Child-Centred Practice for Safeguarding and Child Protection
Strategies for Every Early Years Setting
Rachel Buckler

Little Brains Matter
A Practical Guide to Brain Development and Neuroscience in Early Childhood
Debbie Garvey

Creativity and Wellbeing in the Early Years
Practical Ideas and Activities for Young Children
Sonia Mainstone-Cotton

Anti-Racist Practice in the Early Years
A Holistic Framework for the Wellbeing of All Children
Valerie Daniel

Speech, Language and Communication for Healthy Little Minds
Practical Ideas to Promote Communication for Wellbeing in the Early Years
Becky Poulter Jewson and Rebeca Skinner

Speech, Language and Communication for Healthy Little Minds

Practical Ideas to Promote
Communication for Wellbeing in the
Early Years

Becky Poulter Jewson
and
Rebecca Skinner

Routledge
Taylor & Francis Group

LONDON AND NEW YORK

Designed cover image: Isabelle Kempster, age 4 years. Isabelle loves drawing and writing stories and her favourite colour is pink.

First published 2024
by Routledge
4 Park Square, Milton Park, Abingdon, Oxon OX14 4RN

and by Routledge
605 Third Avenue, New York, NY 10158

Routledge is an imprint of the Taylor & Francis Group, an informa business

© 2024 Becky Poulter Jewson and Rebecca Skinner

The right of Becky Poulter Jewson and Rebecca Skinner to be identified as authors of this work has been asserted in accordance with sections 77 and 78 of the Copyright, Designs and Patents Act 1988.

British Library Cataloguing-in-Publication Data
A catalogue record for this book is available from the British Library.

Library of Congress Cataloguing-in-Publication Data
Names: Jewson, Becky Poulter, author. | Skinner, Rebecca (Speech and language therapist), author.
Title: Speech, language and communication for healthy little minds: practical ideas to promote communication for wellbeing in the early years/Becky Poulter Jewson, Rebecca Skinner.
Description: Abingdon, Oxon; New York, NY: Routledge, 2024. |
Series: Little minds matter | Includes bibliographical references and index. |
Summary: — Provided by publisher.
Identifiers: LCCN 2023023207 (print) | LCCN 2023023208 (ebook) |
ISBN 9781032371269 (hardback) | ISBN 9781032371252 (paperback) |
ISBN 9781003335429 (ebook) Subjects: LCSH: Children—Language. | Speech—Study and teaching (Early childhood) | Language acquisition. | Interpersonal communication in children. Classification: LCC LB1139.L3 J484 2024 (print) | LCC LB1139.L3 (ebook) |
DDC 372.62/2—dc23/eng/20230802
LC record available at https://lccn.loc.gov/2023023207
LC ebook record available at https://lccn.loc.gov/2023023208

ISBN: 978-1-032-37126-9 (hbk)
ISBN: 978-1-032-37125-2 (pbk)
ISBN: 978-1-003-33542-9 (ebk)

DOI: 10.4324/9781003335429

Typeset in Optima
by Deanta Global Publishing Services, Chennai, India

Contents

Foreword

The next book in our Little Minds Matter series is *Communication and Interaction for Healthy Little Minds*, focusing on speech, language and communication. We know that concerns around children's speech, language and communication are increasing for many practitioners, and we were so keen to have a book helping us all to understand how we can support children and their families in this area.

Becky and Rebecca share with us their knowledge and practice and, at the beginning of the book, offer us helpful indicators of development around speech and language which I know many will find extremely beneficial. Throughout the chapters, ideas and suggestions are provided, including how we can use active listening skills, with tips on how to use these skills, what 'active listening' means and how it can support the child's communication. The book also explores speech, language and communication needs, offering ideas on how we can support these needs by considering different communication tools and a range of practical support.

The in-practice experience of Becky and Rebecca is also shared, using case studies to highlight examples of both their own and others' experience. These include stories from parents – one focusing on a child with selective mutism, which is a powerful and insightful read of an issue that, in my experience, we are increasingly seeing.

As with the other books in our series, there are many opportunities for the reader to stop and reflect on their practice. Once again, this is a book which can be used for an individual's professional practice and reflection; or it can also be used as part of a team's professional practice.

I think this will be such a useful addition to everyone's library, offering us all ideas that we can come back to time and again.

Sonia Mainstone-Cotton
Series Adviser
April 2023

Acknowledgements

Well, where do we start? We are so fortunate to be in environments of true connections and love, where we are supported, understood and helped along our journey. So probably the best place to start is, as always, with the children. We really do find it an absolute privilege to be invited into their communications, their play and their lives. The children have placed their trust in us and in turn we can connect and learn together.

Thank you to the educators and parents who invite us into their lives to work with them, and to develop a deeper understanding of communication and emotional wellbeing with their children, families and teams.

We would like to say a massive thank you to the parents, educators and colleagues who took the time to share their experiences and personal stories. We know that for some of you, this was not an easy thing to do; but your voices will be heard and do make a difference. We are truly grateful.

We have an amazing 'village' of people who listen, chat, hug, laugh and reflect with us. Thank you for your wise words and funny one-liners, Gray, Glin, Hils, Ian and Matt. The fabulous Lindy Loo; especially Mindy too; graceful Vane and tasteful Jane; star sis Carina; Leanne, Vicky Mac, Lainey and Lynne – educators extraordinaire. And Cathy and Sam, who have made the most amazing leap into early years.

Thanks to Sue, for believing and joining in our advocacy for children and their communications. To Kelly and John at facts4life, for working together with us to ensure communication and emotional wellbeing continue to thrive. To the awesome Hub and the inspiring children and families' teams at the University of Gloucester and the University of Worcester; to the wonderful workforce in the café who have supplied us with endless cuppas, gorgeous lunches, chats and big welcoming waves and smiles. These little moments have rallied us along our road of writing and researching our intriguing book.

To Kathy Brodie and Lynnette Brock, thank you for your inspiration, knowledge and belief in us. Your support is always valued.

Thank you to the wonderful Emily, with your amazing knowledge of words, kindness, quick wit, and reining in our love of a semicolon.

To the excellent series adviser Sonia and editor Clare, for your kindness and support – thank you for believing in and strengthening early years through enabling educators to write and share our stories, ideas and research.

Thank you to all our speech and language therapy colleagues: you do a brilliant job, often in challenging circumstances, and your commitment to hearing children and enabling them to be heard however they are communicating is awesome.

Thank you to Tommy Brentnall for your brilliant creativity. Find Tommy at @piggybankshoe (Instagram).

Flowie, Aggie, Lissy, Harry, Lottie, Sophie, Guy, Belle, Billy, Alfie and Vana: thank you for choosing us to spend your childhoods with; for keeping us on our toes and up to our knees in mud and water; for revelling in play; and for all the fun, love and laughter.

Thanks to Shirley, Tony, Dee and Roger – a force to be reckoned with; a gentle giant; a wonder woman; a wise, kind man.

We thank you for the wise words, chilly days, endless opportunities to play, great adventures; being there when we need you; the huge hugs, macaroni cheese and cuppas!

Go out and play, kids, it's raining!

Do your best and be yourself – that's all we can ask for!

Thank you to everyone who continues to help us to create environments where everyone is understood and where communications can thrive. For the adults who listen, who see the importance of each and every communication and interaction, and who connect with others daily to help make lives better.

With love,
The Beckies

In forest school, Becky also goes by the name 'Becky Blue Coat' – thank you Charlie.

In speech therapy, Rebecca also goes by the name 'The Talking Lady' – thank you children.

Introduction

Early years professionals have a duty of care to respond to all non-verbal and verbal communication. It is vital that we create environments where all children are understood, no matter how they are communicating.

The key role of the early years professional is to understand the child; their communication, their play, their emotional and physical wellbeing. We do this through Listening, Observing, Valuing and Engaging!

The research tells us that children with language difficulties at age five were:

- four times more likely to have reading difficulties in adulthood;
- three times as likely to have mental health problems; and
- twice as likely to be unemployed when they reached adulthood (Law et al 2020).

By understanding how adults can promote children's health and wellbeing in the early years, we can support children with techniques and strategies which will promote emotional regulation, resilience, and an understanding of emotions and how they can impact us physically.

There is an awareness in the early years sector that behaviour is communication but there is still a deeper understanding that is needed in order to interpret this behaviour and know 'where next', especially when supporting children with speech, language and communication needs.

This book aims to introduce educators to current research in the field of health and wellbeing in the early years and how this links to speech, language and communication and will also provide ideas that can be used in practice including practical ideas to support emotional wellbeing and communication development.

DOI: 10.4324/9781003335429-1

Emotional wellbeing is so closely linked to communication and 'having a voice'; this book will support educators to reflect on their setting and the children in their care and to ensure that they have a clear understanding of each child's unique personality and communication skills.

Case studies and opportunities to reflect on practice mean that this book is accessible, relevant and easy to dip in and out of.

Our aim is that educators reading this book will develop a greater understanding of communication, interaction and emotional wellbeing and that they will discover ways to enable these areas to thrive in their settings.

Every child in our care and education will have different life experiences. Our role is to respond to each individual child with professional love and responsive communication. Early years practice without judgement is essential if we want children to know that they are safe with us and that they really do matter!

Communication and connection

What is communication?

This sounds like an easy question to answer, but communication is so much more than just talking.

The *Oxford English Dictionary* defines 'communication' as:

> *The activity or process of expressing ideas and feelings or of giving people information.*

Let's unpick this a little more. Communication is the process by which information, ideas and messages can be shared between individuals or groups of people. This can be achieved by speaking and listening; or by writing letters, emails or texts. Communication can also occur through visual systems such as social media – we can interpret a message by looking at a photo that somebody has shared on the internet.

We communicate how we are feeling through our body language and non-verbal actions; and we can express whether we are ready to engage with another person through our eye contact and how we position ourselves.

DOI: 10.4324/9781003335429-2

'Communication' can be summarised as the transfer of information from one individual to another or to a group of others. This transfer of information implies a dynamic process, but this is not always deliberate or conscious.

 MINDFUL MOMENT...

Think about a time when you were tired, angry, frustrated or fed up. Did anybody approach you and ask if you were feeling okay? Did they comment on how tired you look? Did you notice that they seemed to be giving you space or keeping their distance?

It is possible that you were expressing your feelings and emotions non-verbally through your body language, but you may not have been aware of this. Those of us working with children will be very aware that all behaviour is communication. We talk about this frequently when trying to understand the children we are working with; but we can sometimes forget that our own behaviour is also communication. We will explore our own communication styles later in this book, but we wanted to plant this seed of reflection early on!

Communication is the process of sharing information with a person or group of people.

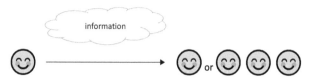

The many ways in which we communicate

Verbal

Here we are referring to spoken language. This obviously includes the words and the language being spoken; but we must also consider how the spoken language is delivered – tone, pace, formal or informal language. Think about how you speak in an important meeting or a job interview and then consider how you 'chat' with friends and family: do you notice any differences?

Non-verbal

We have already touched on this, but think about posture, facial expression, eye contact and eye movements. Think about eye rolling: it is easily done without much thought, but how do we feel if we see someone roll their eyes after something we have said or done? It doesn't make us feel good about ourselves. We use gesture to communicate: we point to direct another person's attention to something we are interested in or to show them where to go; we wave to say goodbye; we might offer a thumbs-up or a high-five to communicate celebration or success – the list goes on!

Sign language – in Britain, British Sign Language – was officially recognised as a language by the UK government in 2003. It is a visual means of communicating through the use of gestures, facial expressions and body language. It has its own grammar and sentence structure, and is mainly used by people who are deaf or have a hearing impairment. For more information, visit www.british-sign.co.uk.

Other systems exist to support language, such as Makaton, which is commonly used in Britain and is a system of signing a key word alongside spoken language. With Makaton, signs are used with speech, in spoken word order. This helps to provide extra clues about what someone is saying. Using signs can help people with no speech or whose speech is very unclear. For more information, visit www.makaton.org.

Visual

We mentioned social media earlier: like it or loathe it, social media has enabled a system of visual communication which facilitates interaction across the world. There are also other systems of visual communication which provide us with information – think of maps, charts and graphs.

Written

Written communication can take the form of letters, emails, texts and so on. How many of us leave little notes for our colleagues or write observations in setting to share with parents/carers?

Why do we communicate?

Humans are inherently social, so communication is essential to our humanity.

> *It is important to our expression and self-determination as individuals, our sense of belonging within a community, our inclusion and participation within society, and in acknowledging the meaning and value of ourselves and others.*
> McEwin & Santo 2018

When we reflect, we can start to see the many different reasons why we communicate. We will explore these in more detail shortly; but first, let's consider why communication matters.

Communication is a social activity – we cannot have society or civilisation without the ability to communicate with one another.

Evans (2021) summarises the importance of communication:

> *Good communication prevents wars and misunderstandings, helps us meet our needs, establishes rules and laws that aid in the structuring of society, helps*

people find and keep employment, provides information and guidance to people, and passes down cultural traditions, norms and values.

This is powerful stuff – the importance of communication cannot be overstated.

So, how is this relevant to those of us working in early years? Well, we are educating and understanding children at a period of their life when their brains are growing at their fastest rate (see Chapter 2 for more details). As a result, we have a duty of care to understand all children, however they communicate; and we must support them in developing their communication skills to enable them to be part of their community and contribute to the society to which they belong. No pressure, then!

Let's return to thinking about **why** we communicate. There are many different reasons for communicating, and it is important to think about these so that we can ensure we are supporting all children in fully expressing their needs, wants and preferences.

To provide information and share ideas

Think about how we receive information in our daily lives: through the news, announcements on social media, books such as this one. Information is communicated to us in many different ways and in many different styles.

We communicate with parents/carers information about dropping off and picking up times and processes. We hold parent consultations so that we can share information about a child's developmental progress.

We communicate with the children in our settings to share information about the world around us and support their learning. We communicate about the routine of the day; and often we do this visually to support understanding of what will happen next and later in the session.

To seek information

We use our communication skills to ask questions. We might need to ask for directions if we are going to a new place or for clarification if we haven't understood something. Children are natural questioners – think about the typical 'Why?' phase. Children need to ask questions to further their learning. We must respect this and offer the answers; and if we don't know the answers, we must model how to research and find the information required. This could be through books, the internet or asking someone else who may have the information needed.

To express emotions

We communicate to express our emotions; and as we mentioned earlier, this may not be a conscious action. There are so many emotions: we communicate joy, fear, anger, satisfaction, disappointment, excitement – the list goes on. There will be times when children and colleagues are expressing their emotions and may need support from us in regulating these emotions if they are feeling overwhelmed. This is where we can offer them a bit of ourselves and co-regulate with them. We do not need to fix the situation, but we do need to show them that we are there and they are safe. We will explore emotional regulation in more detail in Chapter 2.

To make and maintain relationships

We are social beings. As a species, we have survived by living in social groups and working together. We communicate to develop connections with others and we do this by:

- Sharing experiences and interests.
- Showing compassion and empathy.
- Giving support and reassurance.
- Offering advice and guidance.
- Having fun and laughing together.

To express a need, desire or preference

This is different from seeking information. We also communicate to have our physical and emotional needs met – for example, asking for a drink, for something to eat or for company.

To persuade and motivate

Consider advertising campaigns designed to persuade you to buy a specific item, or a politician on a campaign rally communicating their policies and ideas to gain votes.

MINDFUL MOMENT...

Do you use communication to persuade/motivate in the early years environment? Think about your setting and your practice: have you found yourself trying to persuade a child to eat their lunch or use the toilet? We are in positions of power, and we must be mindful about this and reflect regularly to find a good balance where children feel that they have power and influence in their environment.

What does it mean to communicate?

We have explored the various ways in which we communicate and the many reasons why we need to communicate; but we also want to consider for a moment what it means to us as humans to be able to communicate. In order to reflect on this, we wanted to share the following case study with you, as it gives us some insight into how it feels when communication becomes impaired.

CASE STUDY

Roger has been treated for Parkinson's disease for the last 15 years and is experiencing changing communication skills:

My speech is slurred and has a lack of clarity. It feels as if my mouth and lips are swollen; as if I have been to the dentist. My voice is very quiet, and it is very tiring trying to talk.

I often get asked to repeat what I've said and it feels like I am excluded from any conversations, particularly in a group situation.

It is very frustrating when I can't communicate effectively.

This insight is important. We strive to hear the voice of the child no matter how they are communicating, but it is very difficult to explore how it feels as a child or young person when communication is difficult. Quality research in this area is limited, but we can turn to the adult population to learn how communication difficulties impact on emotional wellbeing.

Earlier in this chapter, we listed the various reasons why we communicate. Just pause for a moment to think how difficult it could be for Roger to do any of those things with his communication challenges. Take a moment also to consider what might be helpful for individuals who are trying to express themselves when facing communication difficulties. We will explore this further in Chapter 3.

What happens in our brains and bodies when we communicate?

The process of understanding language and expressing our thoughts, feelings and needs is a complex one. We have included a diagram to help explain it; but first, let's consider communication from an anatomical and physiological perspective.

Language – 'a communication system composed of specific elements' (Atkinson and McHanwell 2002) – is governed by a set of rules which must be followed in order for the communication to be successful. These rules determine the meaning of words (semantics) and the order of words in a sentence (syntax); while linguistic rules ensure that speech sounds, sign language, gestures used to communicate and the written word are interpreted in the brain so that we can understand the intended message.

Our brains also use these rules to construct a reply – whether this be through spoken words, in writing or through sign language.

Broca's area and Wernicke's area are parts of the brain which are vital for language comprehension and expression, as well as for speech production.

Broca's area, located in the frontal cortex, is believed to play a major role in the production of speech and written language. The brain transforms language concepts into motor signals, which then activate the motor cortex to create the output.

Wernicke's area, located in the temporal lobe, is believed to play an active role in the comprehension of language (processing and understanding) (adapted from Stinnett et al 2021).

We have clearly simplified this explanation of the brain function required for communication – we could write a whole book on what happens in the brain when we communicate!

It is interesting to consider which parts of our brain play a significant role in communication; but we think it may be more useful to break things down further and consider what has to happen in order for us to listen and speak.

What happens when we listen and speak?

We have created a simple model to illustrate the steps involved in listening to an instruction/comment and forming a response. Based on a model originally shared by Stackhouse and Wells (1997), this diagram reveals that communicating is a complex process.

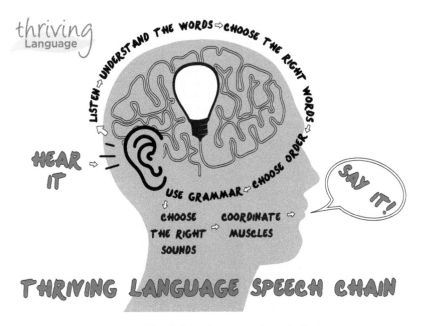

Figure 1.1 The Thriving Language Speech Chain

Let's work through each step in turn …

- **Hear:** In order to hear language, we need to have working ears. Our ears pick up sound waves carried by the air. The middle part of the ear amplifies the sound waves and the inner part of the ear converts this energy into electrical activity. The brain receives this electrical activity via auditory pathways and recognises it as sound, which is then decoded and interpreted.

  Some children have glue ear, which can affect their ability to hear clearly. Glue ear happens when the middle ear becomes filled with sticky fluid. Common signs of glue ear include behavioural changes; tiredness and frustration; lack of concentration; playing alone; and not responding when their name is called. As a result, children with glue ear can be misunderstood or labelled 'difficult' (www.ndcs.org.uk).

  If you are working with a child with hearing impairment or deafness, you will need to adapt your communication to ensure that they can access the message you are conveying.

- **Listen:** Even with working ears, some children find it hard to listen. To listen effectively, a child needs to be able to focus on what is being said to them and filter out background noise. They need to be able to identify what is a person's voice and what is background noise.

- **Understand the words:** The child needs to work out what has been said – what does it mean? Is it an instruction? Do they need to reply?

- **Choose the right words:** The child knows they need to reply; they then need to work out what they want to say (vocabulary). What combination of nouns, verbs and adjectives should they choose?

- **Choose the right order:** For example, 'I would like milk, please,' NOT 'Milk I please like would.' Children need to plan the sequence of the words in their response to ensure that it makes sense to the other person.

- **Use grammar:** The little details of language – for example, 'I would like milk, please,' NOT 'I would liking milk please.'

- **Choose the right sounds:** The child needs to know which sounds make up the words they wish to say.

- **Coordinate muscles:** A message is sent from the brain to the mouth, which instructs the lips, teeth, tongue and soft palate (articulators) where they need to be positioned to produce a sound. This is a process of coordinated movement and in order to produce this output, we need a source of energy.

- For all sounds in the English language, the energy needed is sourced from air in the lungs (exhalation). Air travels from the lungs through the larynx (the structure in the throat which houses the vocal cords). The vocal cords open and close in order to produce vowels and voiced consonants (eg, b, d, g, v); this process is called phonation. The stream of air is then modified by the articulators listed above.
- **Say it:** This process explains how we communicate through the spoken word. For children who communicate through sign, the brain and body progress through the same stages until the final stage above, where the coordination of muscles refers to the hand movements and facial expressions associated with sign language.

As we mentioned earlier, this is a complex process; and it is unsurprising that for some children, the process can break down. We will explore communication difficulties in more detail in Chapters 3 and 4.

Communication milestones

Each child is unique and will develop and grow in their own way. We wanted to set out some key 'milestones' for communication development, as understanding developmental norms is essential when working with children; but please be mindful not to use this as a checklist.

By 6 months

Listening and attention

- Turns towards sound.
- Recognises a key adult's voice.

Social interaction

- Smiles when other people smile.

Language

- Different cries for different needs.
- Making sounds – cooing, some babbling.

By 6-12 months

Listening and attention

- Looks at you when you speak or call their name.
- Fleeting attention – the child's attention is held momentarily by the dominant stimulus in the environment but is easily distracted by any new stimulus.

Social interaction

- Early turn-taking – will babble back to an adult when spoken to.
- Makes noises to get an adult's attention.

Language

- Babbling strings of sounds ('ba ba ba').
- First words emerging and often used with gestures – for example, 'up' with arms extended.
- Is beginning to recognise names of familiar objects/people ('ball', 'Daddy').

By 12-18 months

Listening and attention

- May enjoy looking at a book with an adult.

14

- May dance along to music or singing.
- Rigid attention – can focus attention on own play.

Social interaction

- Copies what others are doing and saying – may copy waving goodbye.

Language

- Understands more words than they can say – typically everyday objects (eg, body parts, clothes and furniture).
- Understands simple questions ('Where's Daddy?')
- May say up to 20 single words to request things or to comment on what they can see.
- Spoken words may not be clear.
- May still be babbling as they play. Strings of 'jargon' may sound like they are talking in sentences, but they are not using real words.
- Emergence of simple pretend play (giving teddy a drink, pretending to talk on the telephone).

By 18-24 months

Attention and listening

- Can now concentrate on play for longer.
- Rigid attention – can concentrate for some time on a task of their own choosing. Has difficulty tolerating interventions or interruptions to their play by an adult.

Social interaction

- Lots of copying – sounds and words.

Language

- Understands simple questions and instructions ('Where is your cup?' 'Show me your nose').
- Can now use approximately 50 single words, which are becoming more recognisable to other people.
- Is starting to put words together to form short phrases and sentences – typically two words together ('More juice,' 'Bye, Mummy').

Speech sounds

- Adults can usually understand about 50% of what the child is saying.
- Often misses the ends off words ('juice' may sound like 'joo').

By 2-3 years

Attention and listening

- Can now listen to and remember simple stories.
- Single channelled attention – child may tolerate a well-timed intervention or interruption, but can only cope with doing one thing at a time.

Social interaction

- Is now playing more with other children and starting to share.

Language

- Can understand longer instructions containing two key words ('Where are mummy's shoes?' 'Make dolly jump').
- Can understand simple 'who', 'what', 'where' questions.
- Can now use up to 300 words.
- Forms longer sentences ('Want more biscuits', 'She took my book').
- Asks lots of questions – at this stage, children want to know the names of things so they can learn new words.
- Develops use of verbs (action words) ('run', 'fall').
- Adds an 's' to indicate simple plurals ('books', 'boots').
- May appear to be stammering – at this stage, children often have lots of ideas they want to share, but their language skills are not always ready, which can lead to some 'bumpy' talking.

Speech sounds

- May shorten longer words ('nana' instead of 'banana').
- Are generally understood by other people.
- May struggle with words where sounds are grouped together ('spoon' may be produced as 'poon').

By 3-4 years

Attention and listening

- Can listen to longer stories and answer questions about the story.

- Beginning to control their own attention. Attention is still single channelled, but it can be stopped/ restarted under the child's control without adult support.

Social interaction

- Is starting to plan games with peers.
- Enjoys and engages with make-believe play.

Language

- Understands and uses concepts such as colour, number and time-related words ('yesterday', 'tomorrow').
- Uses longer sentences and links sentences together with words such as 'and' or 'because'.
- Is starting to talk about things outside of the here and now ('I went Nana's house').
- Asks many questions using 'what', 'where', why'.
- Is starting to answer 'why' questions at a basic level.
- Grammar still developing (may use 'runned' instead of 'ran').

Speech sounds

- Generally clear speech but may still have difficulty with certain sounds (see the speech sounds chart below for further details).

By 4-5 years

Attention and listening

- Can listen and follow instructions without having to stop what they are doing – two channelled attention.

Social interaction

- Can now choose their own friends and who they want to play with.
- Can take turns in much longer conversations.

Language

- Understands more complex concepts ('first', 'last') and more difficult prepositions ('above', 'in between').
- Sentences are now well formed but some grammatical details may remain inconsistent ('sheeps' instead of 'sheep').

Speech sounds

- Uses most speech sounds effectively.

Adapted from Speech and Language UK (www.speechandlanguage.org.uk) and Thriving Language (www.thrivinglanguage.co.uk).

Speech sounds

This chart shows the approximate age at which we would expect to hear specific speech sounds.

Age	Sounds you may hear
1:6 – 2:0	m, p, b
2:0 – 2:6	m, p, b, t, d, w
2:6 – 3:0	m, p, b, t, d, w, f, s, y, k, g, h, l
3:0 – 3:6	m, p, b, t, d, w, f, s, y, k, g, h, l, sh, ch
3:6 – 4:6	m, p, b, t, d, w, f, s, y, k, g, h, l, sh, ch, j, z, r
4:6 Onwards	m, p, b, t, d, w, f, s, y, k, g, h, l, sh, ch, j, z, r, th

We would expect all speech sounds to be developed and in use by eight years of age.

As children grow, the way they say a word will naturally change and it is important to remember that making errors is to be expected as a part of typical development.

Adapted from Thriving Language (www.thrivinglanguage.co.uk/speechsounds)

Reflect on behaviour as communication

How do we really understand what children are thinking and communicating?

The simple answer is to get to know the child extremely well, to like and professionally love them, and to think they are amazing and fun to be with. Notice the child; check in with them; smile and empathise with them and their emotional state; respond to them however their communication is presented. There is more information below on practical strategies; but first have a quick read and reflect here, as this could help to open up communication avenues and develop understanding for the child and you as the nurturing educator.

As we know, and as we have heard many times, behaviour is communication. What we see is what the child is trying to tell us – it lets us know how they are feeling at that given time.

There are many thoughts around gentle parenting and differing parenting styles. It is important for us as educators to understand how we were parented and also how the children we nurture are parented. This can enable us to understand the child's behaviours in a holistic manner, where we see the whole child and not just isolated incidents of behaviour. We are all made up of the experiences we have in life, and how we regulate our emotions and express ourselves depends on the people in our lives as we grow. We can learn to regulate our behaviours as we get older; however, if the child has a foundation of understanding, support and love, their behaviour and communication will be valued and this will support emotional wellbeing now and in the future.

As educators, research and understanding must underpin our practice. We also need to reflect on and understand our own biases and experiences, and the influences that these may or may not have on our professional practice.

When we examine parenting styles further, we might recognise our own practice in them. Gentle parenting is akin to authoritative parenting, where there are fair boundaries and discussions. Children who receive this style of nurturing throughout their childhood are more likely to have the secure wellbeing, self-regulation and independent skills needed to cope with life's ups and downs. For further information in this area, head to https://solihullapp roachparenting.com/ – the Solihull Approach to Parenting is a great resource and continuing professional development forum.

Practical strategies – how to interpret behaviours

We know that it can be very difficult to interpret what a child is trying to communicate in a moment of dysregulation. Here are a few tried-and-tested ideas from practice – we hope they help, but remember to ask for help when you need it too.

Be consistently kind and responsive. This approach should be a unified, cohesive one from the whole team in order to be successful. You, your team and all adults will need to be receptive and forward thinking, and know that your practice is steeped in research on the best outcomes for the child.

MINDFUL MOMENT...

Evaluating your practice is extremely important and should be part of your daily research.

This is a quick strategy to embed and can take just five minutes a day. The difference this will make to you, your team and the children in how you understand each other and how you move forward can be so beneficial (Poulter Jewson & Skinner 2022).

The following statements are from early years educators working in a range of settings:

- *Today we tried ignoring behaviour. However, that just seemed to make the situation worse, so we discussed where to go next and will try to be more in tune. We are speaking to the family to see what the child plays with at home and what their response to requests are like at home; this could help us work together.*
- *It all got too loud and shouty. The room looked like chaos and we were trying to get things done for the end of term. We didn't communicate as a team and tried to move the children all together. The little ones took longer to get ready to go outside and the older ones got bored waiting. Tomorrow we will go out once the first children are ready – we can keep in our ratios and the adults need to be aware and ready to go.*
- *The morning worked well – we were really on it and consistent. This afternoon, not all the team were on board; we tried different approaches, and this became confusing. To be honest, we are exhausted and could really do with some help. We will need to evaluate further and really unpick what is happening before the child is distressed and what our responses are, and perhaps think about gaining more training around communication and behaviours.*
- *Tomorrow we are going to name emotions and have flexibility in our practice. We are going to load play with the child's interest in the water and her love of pebbles, and see where this goes.*

These are simple and honest evaluations from practice. Evaluation doesn't need to be fancy – it just needs to be discussed and recorded, so you know where to go next and you can see what has worked and what hasn't.

How to respond and not react

By 'responding', we mean noticing the child before it all gets too much for them – and for the adults. If we react, the situation can escalate into disarray, where everyone becomes frustrated and stops communicating positively. How does this make you and the child feel?

We need to respond to the child when they are dysregulated; however, we cannot expect them to comply with our rules at this moment in time.

By responding, we are understanding and supporting the research that children do not become dysregulated deliberately – their emotion is overwhelming them. This is when they need us to be calm and show up for them. No judgement; no bargains or bribes – they just need us to 'be' and show them we have got them.

Let's look at how we can respond and what this might feel like for the child and for the adults in their life.

Stage 1: Respond by ...

* Being by them or next to them.
* Naming the main emotion ('You look sad,' 'You seem angry,' 'You look worried').
* Telling them that they are safe.
* Giving them a cuddle if they want one.
* Sitting by them if they want you to.
* Giving them space if they want it.
* Ensuring other children are safe if they are hitting out.

At this stage, the child is totally overwhelmed by their emotions.

Stage 2: Respond by ...

- Being mindful if there is a cue the child is giving you.
- Being near the child.
- Telling the child that they are safe, and that they matter.
- Letting them know we all get upset, angry etc.
- Giving them a way back into play.
- Modelling positive body language so that they feel safe.
- Communicating that you know it's hard when we have big emotions that take over.
- Going outside together away from stimulation and in a natural environment.

Stage 3: Respond by ...

- Watching for the child's cue and being ready to join them – no judgement.
- Chatting together – telling them about a time you were sad, cross etc.
- Having a cuddle if they want one.
- Discussing what happened ('I know you were so cross' – let the child talk about this).
- Thinking about what might help the next time this happens.
- Identifying what props could be available to support the child.
- Setting fair boundaries ('I know you were angry'; 'I am not for hitting – let's find something you could hit (a cushion, a punch bag etc)'; 'I know you wanted the doll, but Jay wanted to carry on playing with it').

By responding, we are teaching the child that emotions happen; that we all have big emotions; and that you can help them to regulate (by co-regulating with them), and you can both come up with solutions that will help the child feel safe.

Stage 4: Responding and supporting everyday emotions in practice in the play environment

Can you create a space where children who need to express natural emotions can do so? To be honest, this is all children, as we all experience emotional highs and lows throughout our lives as humans. Props that may help could include:

- A punch bag in a space where no one can get hurt.
- Cushions that the children can pummel.
- Areas where they can stomp around and make big noises.
- Physical areas where they can swing their arms around and run (Manners 2019).
- Open the door, so that children can regulate themselves and play where their body and mind need them to.
- Books that include children's interests and talk about emotions.
- Photo books of children's trusted adult – who does the child want in their book?
- Photo book of things that are important to the child – their favourite car, coat, person, animal etc.

Trust children and use your communication style to ensure that they know they are worth listening to however they communicate.

When we talk about all behaviour being communication, this is what we mean. We cannot dismiss or disregard communication because we don't understand it, it overwhelms us or we feel it is wrong and that the child should behave better. Our role as educators is to unpick and analyse what it really feels like for the child to experience these emotional dysregulations, and to offer all the support and help that we can to join with families and take a consistent approach where the child feels safe, has fair boundaries and is responded to with understanding, kindness and the latest research in practice around child development.

It may be that the child feels safe to let their feeling out: they are in a safe space, they know that your reaction will be consistent, and they are containing too many feelings that are just too big to hold in any longer.

Don't worry about trying to fix or distract – the learning and teaching moment is in acknowledging the child's feelings and emotions. They are learning that you are listening to them and you are not ignoring them – you are there for them. This has a powerful meaning for the child: they know that they are safe (Knost, 2013), and their brain can start building the connections needed for co-regulation.

CASE STUDY

Lemmy is an older child in the group who has previously settled. But lately, he has been getting a little more upset each day as he arrives. He came into the setting crying again today – he really didn't want to leave his parent. The team chatted about this and suggested it is because of his attachment. The main educator decided that the best thing to do would be to leave him until he was ready to come into the group to play.

This happened again the next day. Lemmy was sobbing quietly by himself. One educator went over to see if he needed some help. She told him he was safe and that it was okay to be sad. She squatted next to him and offered him a hand to hold; he looked at her and held her hand. She asked him if they could go and find his peg together and he nodded. They went off together hand in hand to find his peg.

MINDFUL MOMENT...

Let's consider the following questions around the case study to unpick responsive active communication and behaviour:

- Do the team know enough about attachment-led practice?
- The lead in the team felt they knew why Lemmy was crying; is this enough? What else could they discuss?
- What would help Lemmy to settle?
- What could help Lemmy and his family?
- If you saw one of your friends crying like Lemmy, what would you do?
- What consistent response could the team use?
- What were Lemmy's emotions communicating to the educators?
- What response do you think you and your team would use for Lemmy?
- What else might help and how would you continue to support Lemmy?

We can also signpost to other professionals such as play therapists who can help children to work through their emotions. If the child's play becomes destructive or aggressive, the play therapist can help the child to continue this play cycle to fruition; they can recognise the importance for the child to communicate in this way. This is a specialist skill and is not part of our role as educators; however, helping a child to name and understand their emotions is an important part of the educator's role.

It is difficult at times to access therapy or help, as waiting lists can be long. It may be worth contacting local charities that fund early intervention for children and that recognise the amazing benefits of supporting children in early years.

Private therapy is available; however, this comes at a cost and is a discussion for each child's family. When you are signposting, look at community interest companies and charities, as these often have a sliding scale of pricing and can often access funding. Other helpful professionals to speak to are community family workers, who often have a wealth of knowledge on where to get help and funding.

Active communication: what does this mean in practice and why does it matter for children's emotional wellbeing?

Children require their educators and the adults in their lives to be interested in them and their ideas. By 'active communication', what we are really saying is: be in the moment with children. Be present and remember that active communication is holistic – it is the whole of you: your face, your expressions, your body language, your positioning, your tone of voice, the level you speak at. There is a wide array of ways in which we communicate; however, being physically and emotionally present for the child can establish a great basis for promoting their wellbeing and their own active communication. To understand how we communicate and how this influences the child's world and their view of themselves, we must first reflect on our own dynamic and active communication styles.

Reflection on practitioner communication styles and their impact on children

How do adults and educators communicate? Do you recognise your communication style? It is sometimes easier to understand other people's communication styles, so looking at this with colleagues and developing understanding together can really help. Here are some examples of different communication styles:

- Chats all the time – about all sorts and everything.
- Excited and joyful – happy to communicate and connect.
- Listens and then adds some of their own ideas.
- Listens and then asks you to extend your thoughts.
- Radiates as they communicate – encompasses others.
- Emotional communicator – understands how self and others feel.
- Emotive communicator – evokes an emotional response.
- Quiet and thoughtful – needs time to process and respond.
- Disengaged – is not interested in the subject matter.
- Engaged – is interested and passionate in the subject matter.
- Expressive – uses gestures, body language and discussions.
- Dysregulated – is unable to respond at the time; may appear to switch off.
- Overwhelmed – is rushed and appears agitated.
- Non-tuned – is not in tune with the pattern of conversation.
- Inconsistent communicator – response will be varied; can appear dismissive.

We often communicate differently in our personal lives from our chosen careers; you may also recognise your partner's or family's communication style from the examples above. With our educator's hat on, we know that our profession is vital in building child communication skills and brain development. Thus, we have a crucial responsibility to respond proactively to children, with time, patience and in an engaged, responsive manner.

The educator's communication style should establish an environment in which children can thrive: where they are listened to, heard and – most importantly – responded to. Recognising our communication style enables us to build on our strengths in practice and to reflect on how we should regulate or stimulate our own responses. There is no stronger element to our practice than kinder education, where joint communication with the child nurtures their confidence and wellbeing, and creates an environment in which the child can express their ideas and in which the educator listens and extends through the child's play and creativeness. The environment really is the teacher; and as you are the environment, your role in this can enable children to thrive now and throughout their future lives.

Wellbeing and communication are key elements in building self-esteem and independence, and bringing joy to the lives of others. What a fantastic person you are for choosing a career that helps thousands of children to express themselves! The seeds that you plant in your practice now will travel far and wide: they will continue to grow long into the future. As the children you work with grow, they will take these seedlings and be able to develop magnificently and spread your teachings. Friedrich Froebel spoke of children as seedlings of nature and we think he is spot on there – head over to the Froebel Trust (https://www.froebel.org.uk/) for more inspiration.

Have you looked at *The Hundred Languages of Children* (Malaguzzi 1996)? If you have, it is always worth revisiting; and if you haven't, you are in for a treat. Discovering how children communicate and express their thoughts is crucial, and the Reggio Emilia approach is great at giving depth to the understanding of what this can look like in everyday practice.

Summary

Communication happens all around us. We use words, signs, images and gestures to express ourselves; and there are many reasons why we communicate. Many of us understand why communication matters, and we have touched on how it feels when that skill is lost due to disease or disability.

It is important that we, as educators, are aware of the role that communication plays in establishing relationships and in creating our identity and sharing it with others.

Children develop their communication skills at different rates; but we have explored what 'typical' language development looks like and what happens in our brains and bodies when we communicate.

We hope that we can all now reflect on the importance of communication and the relationship this has with our emotional wellbeing.

 # Further reading and research ideas

British Sign Language – information and training courses
www.british-sign.co.uk

The Froebel Trust
www.froebel.org.uk

Makaton – information and training courses
https://makaton.org/

National Deaf Children's Society
www.ndcs.org.uk

Regio Emilia approach
https://www.reggiochildren.it/en/reggio-emilia-approach/

Signature – signing information and training
www.signature.org.uk

Speech and Language UK
www.speechandlanguage.org.uk

Solihull Parenting Approach
https://solihullapproachparenting.com/

Thriving Language Community Interest Company
www.thrivinglanguage.co.uk

'Am I safe?'
'Do I matter?'
'Do you hear me?'

'Emotional wellbeing' – this term is used frequently, but do we stop and think about what it really means, and do we apply it to children in the early years?

If you embark on research in this area, it soon becomes clear that there are many definitions and interpretations of this term; but the common theme is having the ability to express and understand the vast range of emotions that we experience.

Many adults still find this skill difficult; so how do we help the children in our care to develop this awareness, understanding and acceptance of their emotions?

We think that a good place to start is with the developing brain. This chapter focuses on the brain to enable us to develop our understanding of the physiology of emotional wellbeing and to recognise the relationship between emotional wellbeing and brain development.

Little minds really do matter, and we have a duty of care to extend our knowledge and reflect on our practice. It is by doing this that we become 'tuned-in adults' who **respond** rather than react to children's needs.

DOI: 10.4324/9781003335429-3

Am I safe?' 'Do I matter?' What do these questions mean?

Have you ever noticed the children you are working with giving you a quick sideways glance? They are seeking connections and reassurance. We also know that every seven seconds or so, young children's brains are asking, 'Am I safe?' 'Do I matter?' (Knost 2013). In fact, children seek connection as part of healthy brain development, which is vital for us as humans.

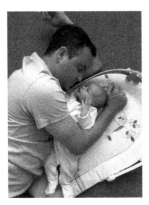

On a very basic level, we need to connect with others to stay safe and to stay alive. There is safety in numbers and our brains are built on the basic instincts that we need to thrive. Suzanne Zeedyk's work brings us back to times of early humans, when we feared sabre-toothed tigers and when people came under real threat every day. These basic instincts are still with us – think fight, flight, freeze and flock, which clearly demonstrate to us how these play out as anxiety in our world today.

As adults, we can often feel dysregulated. We can also see this in children when they are sad, cross or upset; or when they want something or don't want to leave their caregiver. A human's basic need is for connection – without, this they will not thrive (Zeedyk 2020).

Often as teachers, we may have thought that the quick glance from the child was perhaps a distraction, or even a lack of attention or a need for attention. We may have missed the look and later observed the child looking a little distant.

A great way to think about a child needing attention is to flip it around and think about their basic need to connect with you and other people in their lives. For example, we often see siblings who cuddle a lot and give reassurance to each other. They may then need to go off to different classes for the day; but whenever they see each other, they may like to hug. This is a great way to top up their connection levels. If you want to know what co-regulation feels and looks like in practice, the sibling cuddle is a great example.

We have worked in many educational settings where this is allowed to happen, and it is a joy to see. Sadly, however, we have also observed educational environments where this isn't allowed. Think how this would feel! Even as adults, we would find it difficult to see our friend across a room and not connect with them; and we are pretty sure that if someone hurried you along away from your friend, this might make you feel annoyed or sad.

We do understand that children have routines; however, we also need to balance this with their need for connection and the importance that their emotions play in how they communicate their needs to the outside world. If you cannot express how you feel as a young child, when can you express this? We as adults know the importance of being heard and having our feelings validated. However, this does not happen automatically – it is a learned process based on establishing trust, where the responses we receive are supportive and enable our brains to build regulation and resilience.

Resilience does not grow through tough love or ignoring crying, sadness and anger. Sadly, some children do develop resilience due to their circumstances – they realise no one is coming to help, so they try their best to nurture themselves and keep themselves safe. They may see the world very differently from a child who has received co-regulation. Empathy must be seen and modelled often for children's brains to develop in an empathic way (Grimmer 2021).

We as educators are significant adults in many children's lives, and it is extremely important that we know how to co-regulate and recognise this. Overly high expectations of children and their behaviours will only show the children that they are misunderstood and on their own. Validating children's emotions is crucial. You may not be able to solve the problem, and that's okay; however, you can always show genuine empathy for and with the child.

Consider this scenario: a child falls over in the playground and hurts their knee and starts crying, just as they are due to go back inside.

How do we respond?

You could say, 'You look sad – what can I do to help?'

You could say, 'I would be sad too if I hurt my knee.'

You could say, 'Do you need a cuddle?'

Look at the child's body language and see what they are telling you.

We know that when we work with children, some of them will get straight back up from a fall, brush it off and run away – this is their way. But it's still a good idea to check in with them: 'I noticed you fell over – are you okay?' The key communication here is that you have noticed them, and they know that they matter to you.

We know that some children will be shocked when they fall over, and this is what frightens them.

It also often hurts when you fall over, and all children have different tolerances for pain.

As kindly as this is said or meant, 'Jump up and you'll be okay' does not really help the child to communicate how they are feeling.

We want children to talk about their emotions and communicate them to us in the everyday as the norm. Using supportive, empathic communications throughout our practice can help the children to do this naturally.

A child falling over is a prime connection moment to let them know that they are noticed; that they are safe; that they matter; and most importantly, that they are professionally loved (Page 2011). Working with children is a true privilege: we are the connection workers who build the foundations for the next generation. Childhood is a time to be loved; to really know that you matter; to feel safe and be enabled by the adults in your life to thrive.

MINDFUL MOMENT...

We often hear the term 'the unique child' (Early Years Foundation Stage 2021) – what does this really mean to you and each child you work with?

How well do you know and connect with each child? This is a great opportunity to be honest and reflective, and to build stronger connections with children you feel you may not understand or have connected with yet. Like any relationship, building connections takes work and understanding, and will need to be an ongoing process.

Think about each child separately in your practice and ask the following questions, which can help to build a picture of each child's unique journey:

- Am I seen?
- Do I feel loved?
- Am I heard?
- Do I matter?
- Am I safe?
- Do I have the space to thrive and be myself?

A great place to start this reflection is to personally ask yourself these questions too.

The Thriving Language approach highlights the values needed for communication and emotional wellbeing.

© The Thriving Language Approach   © piggybankshoe

Figure 2.1 The Thriving Language Approach for Communication and Wellbeing

Trusting relationships are built on consistency and understanding; only then will a child be ready to learn and start to thrive.

We talk about the importance of research-based practice – by this, we mean what is happening in a child's brain at that very moment. We often change how young children view their world through our reactions and responses. How we choose to respond creates connections and pathways in the child's brain. We want children to know that we are actively listening and observing – that we have them held in mind and that they are important to us.

What and how they feel must be validated, not fixed. We often do not have the ability or power to fix everything; however, we certainly have the superpower of noticing, acknowledging and reassuring. When we do this, the child can start to explore their world with the knowledge that they really do matter. Ta-da! Their brain is now in an optimum space for learning and enquiry with the adults around them, who are consistent and kind teachers.

By consistently and effectively co-regulating with children as they grow, we are teaching them to thrive and enabling them to self-regulate. We all still need co-regulation and connections throughout our lives. If you are feeling overwhelmed, you might chat to a friend or a partner; what you are asking them subconsciously is to help you contain your emotions.

 MINDFUL MOMENT...

Time to head over to the reflection section of your brain

Think of this as a vital time to think. Imagine a cosy area and a cuppa; perhaps even a blanket (make this a reality and really take the time out you need if possible).

This activity can be chatted through with colleagues in a team meeting, done individually, in supervisions or as a whole project on why connections matter. It can take ten minutes; or it can take as long as you have available. The main point is to explore the response and recognition you have towards connections: what your ethos is – and could be – around connection-based practice.

Think of a time in your practice where children have glanced at you:

- How did you respond?
- What could you do to reassure the child?
- How do you connect with children?
- What small gestures could you use?
- Why is it important to create everyday moments of connection-based practice?
- What might happen if connections are often missed?
- If another adult has told a child off and the child is sad, what could you do?
- On a personal note, what enables you to thrive and connect with others?

When children glance at you, this can often be at a time where they are being instructed by another adult – perhaps during circle time or story time. We need to think about how children listen and communicate. If they are looking at you, playing with a toy, twiddling their hair or smiling at their friend, this does not mean they are not listening. Children are active listeners and we need to champion that, as this is how they learn. Sitting for a short period of time if they are engaged is acceptable. However, when we herd children together, this is often when learning goes astray (Bruce 1991). Take a look at all the children's body language and expressions – are they really engaged?

As educators, we should not be using our time to police children's behaviour or to point out who isn't sitting still. We know there is so much more to children than conformity. Think about this for a moment. Most adults know how to sit down – and probably most of us sit down far too much. So, practising a skill that we can all do eventually does need to be questioned and reflected upon. We are pretty sure that if you gave a child an iPad, they would sit down for very long periods of time; this really isn't something we need to strive to master. Dr Lala Manners discusses the connection between physical movement and learning in *The Early Years Movement Handbook*.

As adults, how do we listen? Do we sit perfectly still and look directly at the person who is talking? If we are hearing something new, we might look to the person next to us for reassurance and connect with them to feel like we are all in this together.

Let's explore this a little further. Have you ever been on a training day where you didn't really know anyone; but by the end of it, you had connected with others? How did this make you feel?

Okay, now it's time to flip this around. If, when you tried to connect with another adult through a gesture or a smile, the person you were looking at said, 'Turn around and listen properly,' how would that make you feel? Would it make you feel like you matter and that you are safe? For a start, you might feel that they were being a bit rude; and you most certainly would feel a little shamed, embarrassed, or angry. Would that help you listen; or instead, would you be distracted by how you felt? We always return to research: can children learn and listen when they do not feel connected?

Maslow's Hierarchy of School Needs (as cited by Kurt 2020) outlines the four steps to self-actualisation, when a child is then able to learn. As teachers, knowing this enables us to create environments where we deeply understand how children learn, and where the child feels professionally loved and kept in mind. There is no need for cross voices or scary adults who prevent children from being themselves; we cannot find any research evidence that tells us this helps children to learn.

Children's emotions should be validated and encouraged; and each child should be viewed as an individual. When we create a learning environment with this in mind, children (and adults) can thrive. Time is then spent on teaching and learning, the need for correction is limited and behaviours are viewed as communication. There are fair boundaries, which are research based and which ensure that all who use them feel safe.

MINDFUL MOMENT...

When choosing boundaries and routines, explore both individually and with your team what these would feel like to you. Put yourself in that space and think how they would make you feel.

What is the purpose of the boundaries and how much involvement do the children have in creating and understanding them?

How does the team respond if the boundaries are broken?

- Is this used as a learning and growth moment or is the response a reaction?
- Does the reaction enable the child to thrive?
- What is happening to the child's brain at that moment?
- What is their body language telling you?
- What is your body language telling the children?

What do children need in order to learn and develop?

How important and impactful is your position as an early years educator to the children you work with?

The simple answer here is: 'extremely impactful.' However, there is so much more to your role as an educator. You are crucial, vital, life affirming, life changing; you are a constant; you are a friend, a trusted adult, a relationship builder. All your actions, words and deeds are seen by and modelled to children, and how you see the world is how they will see the world.

So, there is a huge responsibility for educators to get it right, right from the start, and to teach with research, love and kindness running through their practice.

Research boost

What percentage of critical brain development happens in the first five years of life?

1. 50%
2. 70%
3. 90%

You can find the answer at the end of this chapter (source: NSW Health - first 2000 days).

What do children need to learn and develop? This is a big question, and depending on each individual child the answer could be quite different. What we do know is that in early years, we have the freedom to tailor education to child development, and to enable an extremely positive start to life.

This is often the first time that children have experienced being with other adults outside their families, meeting other children and starting their journey to independence. For educators who have chosen a career working with the youngest children, the clear fact is that we are fundamental in creating connections with them. These encompass relationship connections, which in turn develop healthy pathways in the child's brain. Loving professionally (Page 2011), developing a loving pedagogy (Grimmer 2021) and being emotionally available for children are key elements of our practice. We can never underestimate the feeling for a child of being loved and knowing that the adults in their life – including all educators they meet in their educational journey – will respond kindly to their communications and requests, no matter how they communicate.

These communications must be understood and unpicked to give the child the tools to build healthy relationships both today and for their future mental health and their future educational outcomes (Poulter Jewson & Skinner 2022).

By reframing the question, 'What do children need to learn and develop?' and viewing it from the perspective of human relationships and basic needs, it becomes clear that what children need is for you, their educator, to have the time and capacity to understand their emotional make-up alongside their communications. Only when the child is understood, feels safe and knows that they are recognised for who they are in your presence can they truly be themselves and start to engage in their learning and development.

MINDFUL MOMENT...

- How do you learn?
- What makes you feel safe to learn?
- What is your understanding of children's emotional health; their learning and development?
- Do you feel that all children in your care and education have their emotional needs met so that they can learn?
- Have you viewed children who look concerned, worried or upset, and are you enabled to connect with them; or does your routine dictate how and when you connect with children?

Froebel gives us brilliant insight into the purpose of teaching and the education of children from an educator's perspective:

I wanted to educate people to be free, to think, to take action for themselves
Froebel, quoted in Lilley 1967:41

As educators, we must all know why we want to teach. We should have a great personal ethos and research-based beliefs that underpin our teaching. We think it's pretty hard to beat Froebel's philosophy, as this recognises the need for children to believe in themselves and to communicate their ideas.

How does your classroom environment recognise this ethos; and how does it ensure that every adult and child in the setting is part of creating this and understands this?

Kinder education is always the goal. We are responsible for children's mental health and emotional wellbeing both while they are with us and into their future lives.

Are there consequences for children in your setting or teaching environment? Is there still a tendency to give children time-outs? If so, what is the research behind this? Might this make children feel worse about themselves? Do children even know why they are sitting out? This could be for something they did a while ago and they may not even remember the reason. By talking to children when they are calm and regulated, this can be a teaching and wellbeing moment. Remember that young children look to you for how to respond to the world around them. If you teach them when both they and you are calm, the response will be much better.

You will know when young children are ready to learn, as they will be interested and may ask questions or respond to you with positive body language. If children are fidgeting and looking bored, this probably means they *are* bored. We have mentioned above that we are not in the business of shaming children or making them sit still. We are all much better teachers and educators than that; we want to build brains positively and promote robust self-esteem. If children are not learning in the way we want them to learn, then it is up to us to teach in the way that **they** learn. We should seed their play and learning, observe and then extend their thoughts and ideas. It is only once we really understand the child's thinking and learning patterns that we can extend and see the child develop and gain a love of learning and education (Brock 2020; Bruce 1991).

 MINDFUL MOMENT…

What works well when we choose to teach with emotional wellbeing, communication and child development at the heart of our practice?

* Comments rather than questions.
* Genuine interest.
* Open body language.
* A positive atmosphere.
* Validation of emotions.

- Recognition of emotions and when a child has misunderstood.
- Facial expressions – what do they tell the children?

Learning and development: intrinsic and extrinsic praise

Intrinsic self-worth and extrinsic validation – what do these really mean, and why do we need to look further into the emotive nature of star charts and reward systems?

We want children to do things for themselves, not just to please others. If we teach children to be people pleasers and to always conform to others' ideas, what impact might this have on their confidence and their own ideas – both now and in later life? Think back to the Froebel quote and perhaps give it another read. We teach children to think about new ideas based on their interests; we don't teach them what to think (Mead 1973). Our society needs problem solvers and people who believe they have ideas that are worthy of more thought and interest, and who are confident enough to challenge others and themselves. We can gain resilience to persevere from being co-regulated and being allowed to test out our ideas. Things will be tough for children at times; but if they know who to turn to and how to ask for support, this will help them weather the storms of life. They will have a core belief that they matter and that their ideas are worth listening to. They will recognise when to ask for help and when they will be listened to. If children are encouraged to speak up and share their thoughts, this becomes a communication pattern for life.

Intrinsic means being self-motivated and self-encouraged – pleased with themselves for the sake of doing a task, not for the result (eg, an end reward or treat).

Extrinsic means out of self – being affected by what others think and tell us. We are doing something to get a reward. Think of a dog who sits for a piece of sausage.

What does extrinsic praise look and feel like in practice?

> ## CASE STUDY
>
> Joseph is three years old and attends a preschool four days a week in his locality. His family are trying to toilet train him. He doesn't mind sitting on the toilet; his parents remind him often at home to go for a wee. However, he really doesn't like pooing on the toilet. They mention this in his setting and decide to take a combined approach.
>
> The family have a star chart and the nursery chooses the same approach. Dad has said that when Joseph goes to the toilet, they put a star up on his chart and when he has ten stars, he can have a toy. Nursery also creates a star chart to use in the setting and will let Joseph's family know how many stars to add to their chart at picking-up time.
>
> Joseph's key person chats to him about toileting, shows him the toilet and puts his star chart up next to the toilet. He introduces books into the setting that are relevant and that role model toileting. He even finds a funny song about going to the toilet using Facts4Life resources. All these resources are left about in natural play and used for everyday communications.
>
> Joseph tries the toilet a few times and is pleased with himself. His key person says, 'I am so pleased with you for trying the toilet. Your Mum and Dad will be very happy with you.' He encourages Joseph to wash his hands and says, 'Good boy.' He takes a star out and puts it on Joseph's chart.
>
> A bit later in the day, Joseph needs a poo and really doesn't want to go into the toilet area. His key person tells him that if he tries, he can have another star. Joseph reluctantly goes to the toilet area with his key person. His key person brings Joseph's favourite book and reads this to him. Joseph is still a bit frightened, and his key person tries to encourage him: 'Come on, Joseph. You will be able to play after you have a poo and you need more stars so you can choose a new toy.' He

shows him the star chart and they count the stars – only seven more stars to get. Joseph goes back to play not having done a poo and looking a little worried. His key person says, 'Don't worry Joseph – you will get a star next time when you do a poo.'

MINDFUL MOMENT...

- Think about how Joseph might feel.
- What is Joseph's motivation for going to the toilet?
- Reflect on Joseph's emotions and who he is trying to please.
- What works well in this case study?
- How could we develop practice that would enable Joseph to feel empowered?
- What could the practitioner do to validate Josephs emotions?

Toileting is an everyday occurrence – how do we enable this naturally in practice so that it is not highlighted as a problem area?

What happens when a present has been bought for Joseph or when he wets or poos himself?

Now let's explore intrinsic confidence building in practice ...

CASE STUDY: ALTERNATIVE VERSION

Joseph is three years old and attends a preschool four days a week in his locality. His family are trying to toilet train him. He doesn't mind sitting on the toilet; his parents remind him often at home to go for a wee. However, he really doesn't like pooing on the toilet. They mention this in his setting and decide to take a combined approach.

Joseph's key person chats to him about toileting, shows him the toilets and introduces books into the setting that are relevant and that role model toileting. He even finds a funny song about going to the toilet using Facts4Life resources. All these resources are left about in natural play and used for everyday communications. Joseph tries the toilet a few times and is pleased with himself. His key person observes to Joseph that he looks pleased with himself. He encourages Joseph to wash his hands.

A bit later in the day, Joseph needs a poo and really doesn't want to go into the toilet area. His key person reassures him and they go to the toilet area together. His key person brings Joseph's favourite book and reads this to him. Joseph is still a bit frightened, and his key person recognises this: 'You look worried, Joseph.' He names emotions and tells Joseph he is safe. Joseph goes back to play not having done a poo, but a little less worried.

Reflective questions on building intrinsic self-confidence:

Using the above observation of practice, what can we learn about the key person's approach?

- Notice that the key person does not praise Joseph.
- He does not say that he is pleased with Joseph, as Joseph does not need to try to please him.
- He states to Joseph, 'You looked pleased with yourself.' This builds intrinsic self-recognition and self-worth.
- The key person recognises the changes in Joseph's emotions and names them. He doesn't just focus on happy emotions; he discusses 'worried' and 'frightened', and tells Joseph that he is safe. This gives Joseph the words, reassurance and understanding to explore sharing his emotions.
- The key person creates a safe environment for Joseph to communicate. He is aware of non-verbal communications and views these as crucial to understanding child development.
- The key person integrates the key practice for communication of time, space and pace (Skinner and Poulter Jewson, 2022).

The brainy bit: neuroscience and the early years

What is neuroscience?

Put simply, neuroscience is the study of the brain and the nervous system. The part of the nervous system that we are interested in is the central nervous system (CNS), consisting of the brain and the spinal cord.

Mine Conkbayir – an advocate for applying an understanding of neuroscience in the early years setting – describes the CNS as a mechanism to 'coordinate our perception of, and responses to, stimuli in the environment' (Conkbayir 2017).

Being able to do this means that we can scan our environment and be aware of any risks in order to keep ourselves safe.

When does the brain start growing?

Brain development begins shortly after conception and is a complicated process. There is a wealth of research which tells us that the infant brain develops and grows more rapidly from birth to the age of five years than at any other stage in life, so the importance of the role of the early years educator cannot be overstated (Zeedyk 2020). Many of us working in the early years environment understand and appreciate the importance of quality early years care and education, and we need to respect the role that we play in shaping children's developing brains.

MINDFUL MOMENT...

Take a moment to reflect: to what extent do you think about the child's developing brain and what is happening to this fascinating structure when you interact and educate children in your setting?

Neurons and mirror neurons

Neurons are a type of cell that connect and work together to create a complex system of communication. The primary function is to pass messages from the brain to the rest of the body and from the body back to the brain. Essentially, neurons are the building blocks for all our thoughts and actions.

Mirror neurons are fascinating – they are activated when we observe another person carrying out an action and at times result in us unconsciously copying or 'mirroring' that action.

MINDFUL MOMENT...

Think about when you see another person yawn: what often happens?
What about when you see another person eat a super-sour sweet?
Do you open your mouth when the baby you are feeding opens their mouth?
Do you wince when you see someone get a paper cut?

These mirror neurons support us in developing empathy and understanding of other people's feelings and needs – important foundation skills needed in order to build relationships and connections with others.

The limbic system

The limbic system refers to structures in the brain which support the functions of behaviour, memory and emotional development and understanding. Two key parts of the limbic system that we will explore are the hippocampus and the amygdala:

- The hippocampus plays a crucial role in creating and storing memories. It is also vital for learning and regulating emotions and emotional responses (for feeling and reacting).

- The amygdala is responsible for scanning for threats – it plays a key role in assessing dangers and challenges in the environment, and works to plan an appropriate action or response. The amygdala is essential for feeling certain emotions and perceiving them in others, including fear and the changes it elicits in the body.

The brain and language development

Being able to communicate our thoughts, ideas and feelings is essential for our emotional wellbeing. To be heard and understood contributes significantly to the feeling of being valued for who you are. We will explore communication and wellbeing in more detail in Chapter 3.

The limbic system and communication

Two parts of the brain – Broca's area and Wernicke's area – are responsible for the expressive and receptive language skills needed to communicate effectively. However, as we mentioned earlier, they will only thrive and strengthen with quality interactions from others.

So, what about the limbic system? Well, we know that emotions can be expressed non-verbally – think of body language and facial expressions. When we are considering emotional wellbeing, we need to support the child's developing brain in learning the vocabulary which will help them to identify their feelings and then communicate to seek help, comfort or resolution.

MINDFUL MOMENT...

Take a moment for honest reflection – can you think of a time when you have used non-verbal communication to express an emotion to a child in your setting?

- What happened to trigger your non-verbal communication?
- What did you do?

- How did the child react?
- What did the child learn from your non-verbal communication?
- Would you do anything differently next time?
- What would the child gain if you used words?

We know that the limbic system is responsible for the fight, flight, freeze and flock responses; and we know that if a child is too busy scanning their environment in order to feel safe, they will not be able to access all the play and learning opportunities available.

Children need 'tuned-in adults' who are responsive and not reactive, and who can create safe spaces for them to learn and develop.

Why do we need to know about the brainy bit?

We hope that you can already see how the structures of the brain are directly linked to our emotions and behaviours. Stimulating awareness and thought about the 'physiology of emotions' is important because we know that most brains have the same structures, but the growth, development and function of those structures will be influenced by the life experiences of the child. We as educators, along with parents and society as a whole, have the power to shape a child's brain; and we can also influence the type of person the child will turn out to be (Elliott 1999). So let's get it right and support our children to develop their brains in the best possible way.

Every child in our care and education will have different life experiences and we need to respond to each individual child with professional love and without judgement – essential if we want children to know that they are safe with us and that they matter.

Dr Bruce Perry – a psychologist whose work has raised awareness and knowledge of the impact of childhood trauma on brain development – shares with us that:

In order to most efficiently influence a higher function such as speech and language … the lower innervating neural networks must be intact and well regulated.

Perry 2009

What Perry is telling us here is that we need to understand that the emotion centres of the brain must be regulated in order for children to be able to learn. We as educators must know this: we need to be able to recognise and identify opportune moments for 'teaching', and also when our role is to support the emotion centres of the brain and help the child by co-regulating with them.

What is emotional regulation?

Think about a time when you were fully immersed in something you really like doing: perhaps a time when you were cosy and totally relaxed – maybe after a walk in the rain, when you had got back home, got changed, snuggled up and had a warming drink. You had nothing else to do apart from be in the moment and enjoy the time you had to yourself.

Now, picture your brain working calmly and being able to think things through; so if something unexpected happened, such as you spilling your cuppa on the floor, you could deal with it easily. Yes, it might be annoying; but you don't let it escalate – you sort it and you move on.

Being emotionally regulated doesn't mean that you will never come up against any difficulties in life; what it does mean is that you will be able to know how to ask for help and where and when to get any support you feel you need. Emotional regulation could mean that you sit with how you are feeling and reflect on this. It is knowing that you may feel better if you talk to a friend. An example of this could be that you can be really honest about a difficult situation – even though you may feel nervous talking about it, you know that something needs to be done and you can then return to your emotional equilibrium.

When you are emotionally regulated, you are in a good place to think about ideas and resolve difficulties; you can take on board others' ideas and discuss them with confidence. Other people can share their thoughts with you knowing that you will listen and give emotionally intelligent responses. You are confident enough in your own self that you can help others to grow and develop, and know that this will enhance your life and theirs.

Someone who is emotionally regulated responds rather than reacts to everyday life. They tolerate disappointment and express how it makes them feel. They can share their joy and read other people's emotional cues and respond to them with empathy and understanding. They will not try to fix problems and will not manage people's behaviours; they are more likely to respond to the emotion of the situation and voice the other person's feelings. For example, they may notice that a colleague doesn't seem themselves, so they say, 'Are you alright today? You look a little sad.' This emotional intelligence leads to effective co-regulation.

Self-regulation and co-regulation

Birth to Five Matters (Early Years Coalition, 2021) highlights the importance of respectful and 'tuned-in' adults in the development of self-regulation:

> *Self-regulation … is a process that grows out of attuned relationships where the caregiver and baby or child are closely attentive to each other and engage in sensitive, responsive exchanges.*

Self-regulation is the ability to manage our feelings, thoughts, emotions and behaviour, and to be able to regulate them. This is a skill which requires time, support and practice to develop; and many adults still struggle to self-regulate at times of stress. Self-regulation is such an important skill for all of us.  When we can self-regulate, we can think clearly and carefully, and respond to a situation rather than reacting.

The ability to self-regulate has a positive impact on relationships, as we are better placed to manage conflict and challenges. We will develop stronger resilience in the face of difficulties, such as a tricky piece of work or task; and we will be able to apply strategies such as taking a deep breath when we experience big feelings, such as fear or anger.

This skill continues to build and grow throughout our lives as we experience different life events. It is important to know that it is not something we achieve in childhood and tick a box, thinking, 'Yes, I can self-regulate now – I can now manage all that life throws at me.' If only it were that simple!

As we mentioned earlier, self-regulation grows from positive relationships. Warm and responsive interactions between adult and child will enable the child to understand their emotions and support them in managing their feelings and behaviours. Consider for a moment: what is our natural instinct when we hear a baby cry? We pick them up, hold them close to us (with some research suggesting we automatically hold them to the left side of our chest, where our heart is), and we gently rock or sway with them. Rhythm regulates the brain (Perry 2009); when we do this, we are literally calming the brain and working with the baby to help them to regulate. We are giving some of ourselves here – we are co-regulating with them.

Children will typically look to other people to work out how to be in a situation and how to feel safe. Early years educators are essential in supporting the development of self-regulation through their ability to co-regulate. Early years educators are 'connection workers', and the importance of this must be acknowledged and understood.

Responsive and kind people are the most powerful tools in helping us to develop our self-regulation skills. It really is all about connection and relationships.

'Love is the antidote to fear' – this has been said by many people throughout history. If you think about this message from an emotional regulation perspective, we can now add meaning to that statement and understand what our role is in enabling the children in our settings to feel safe and that they matter to us. We can take this one step further and also know that by doing this – enabling a feeling of safety – our children can use their brains for development and learning, rather than their brains firing up to keep them safe.

It matters how you are – you cannot co-regulate if you are in a state of fight, flight, or freeze.

What happens to our brains and bodies when we are dysregulated?

We literally flip our lids in our brain (Siegel 2012). We may cry to regulate ourselves; we might shout and scream, or stamp our feet; we might want to get away from everyone; we might need a big hug; we might not be able to function and just freeze or sleep if our emotions are overloaded and we need to shut down.

The adult or child is now functioning in their primitive non-thinking brain, so there is no point asking them to do anything; there is no point telling them off; there is no point continuing to talk to them. Stopping or calming down is not an option. The dysregulated brain is not calming down for anyone or anything for at least 20 minutes.

So, what can we do? We can offer a hug; we can offer a blanket or a comforter; we can offer physical activity, as this is a great way to reset our brain and soothe our emotions by getting rid of excess cortisol and adrenaline (Watkins 2022). We can offer outside play – in nature, our brains become more regulated than in an overstimulating environment. Our role as the secure adult is to help the child regain control and enable them to be co-regulated by borrowing some of our regulation. This is over to us, as connection creator educators. We need to have oodles of self-regulation – children are literally giving us some of their dysregulation they cannot cope with. They are non-verbally, and often verbally, asking us to help them cope.

You may observe the frustration that is overwhelming the child: they cannot hold this and will communicate this through their behaviours. The child is communicating what they feel by subconsciously sharing their feelings with you. We can co-regulate with children when we are regulated ourselves; so, take a breath and look at the emotions and communications behind the behaviours you see. Validating emotions is essential. We cannot just tell a child to stop crying – they can't stop. And if they do stop crying when you tell them to, we need to ask: what is the message they have just received? Is it that they are scared, so they stop; or that they hide their emotions? Either way, this will not enable the child to co-regulate; it only means they have internalised their feelings and feel that they do not matter. Their feelings will still need to come out; however, this could be in a more harmful way for the child as they grow. Worryingly, over 25% of 14-year-olds are thought to have self-harmed (Be Headstrong UK).

Let's look at what we can do in everyday practice:

- We cannot make demands of children who are dysregulated. They have already demonstrated to us that they are finding it all too much (the reason for their dysregulation may not always make sense to us), and they need our help.
- Notice the child, validate their feelings and be child centred in your educational approach.
- Co-regulate – we need to help children of all ages by being kind, under-standing and consistent.
- A child is only able to learn when they feel safe and secure, and when they know they matter to you. Children must know they matter to us and feel safe, however they may be communicating.
- Use fair boundaries, such as: 'I know you are angry. I am not for hitting – you can hit this pillow instead.' We are not trying to mask the actions, feelings or behaviour; we are trying to find a connection and an outlet.
- Children learning about their emotions is a crucial lesson and should be an integral part of our natural teaching.
- Remember, educators are only human (even though you a have super-human career!). If you need a break, take one, regulate and return refreshed.
- Ensure that the day is evaluated and the findings are written down. This need only take five minutes at the end of the day. You might want to answer a few simple reflective questions: how do you feel? What worked? What didn't work? What do you need more help with? What was your best teaching moment of the day? What was your worst teach-ing moment?
- Ensure that you have regular supervision and time to express your reflections. Educators who do not take the time for welfare and wellbe-ing for themselves are unknowingly perpetuating a culture of being too busy for self-care. This in turn will not help set a positive environment for them or the adults and children they work with.
- All behaviour is communication. Our routines and expectations of chil-dren should have co-regulation and kinder education at their core.

MINDFUL MOMENT...

Here are some thoughts that you might like to reflect on and add to. Be as honest as you can – that way, change can start to happen and you can continue your professional journey to deeper emotional connections and understanding.

- The child is changing the atmosphere.
- It is so much easier when the child is not in.
- The team and I are becoming anxious before the child arrives.
- Are all adults using the same connection and regulation approach?
- Where can we go to ask for more help?
- Are we working with the family? Have we asked what happens at home when the child is dysregulated?
- Could we do a home visit to develop deeper connections with the child and their family?
- Do we have long periods of time when the child can play and engage in their interests?
- Do we know what patterns of play and interests the child has and are these understood?
- Do we need more training that will help us to understand where to go next and what we could do for the child?
- Do we love the child professionally? What does this look like and feel like in our setting?
- What are we trying to teach and why?
- What is our flexible routine and are the children at the heart of this?
- What is our ethos and mission statement? Is this how we practice?

What happens to our communication skills and how we interact with others if we are not emotionally regulated?

MINDFUL MOMENT...

Take a moment to reflect. Think of a time when you have been really excited and wanted to tell some exciting news to a friend:

- What happened to your breathing?
- What happened to your body language?
- Did your rate of speech change?
- What happened to the pitch of your voice?
- How did the conversation flow?

Now, if you feel comfortable to do so, think about a time when you were worried, nervous or feeling anxious. Think about your communication skills:

- What happened to your breathing?
- Did your body language change and if so, how?
- What happened to the quality of your voice? Did your voice feel tight and strained?
- What happened to the volume of your voice?
- Were you able to express what you were feeling and thinking? What did you say?
- How did the other person respond/react? And how did this response/reaction make you feel?

We have deliberately picked two contrasting emotions for you to reflect on here. We wanted to share Dr Sophie Mort's (2021) thoughts on emotions – she explores the common categorisation of emotions as either 'good' or 'bad', but stresses that we must accept all emotions without judgement and understand that the physiological changes that often result from these emotions can significantly affect our communication skills.

Think about the 'mindful moment' above and consider how these physiological reactions link to the speech chain we detailed in Chapter 1. We know that we need steady and controlled breath support in order to produce clear speech; so if our heart rate increases due to the emotions we are experiencing, our rate of breathing will likely increase. As a result, we may run out of breath when we are talking; or the breathlessness we are feeling may lead to greater feelings of anxiety.

We also need good breath support to speak with volume. So, if our breathing is impacted by the emotions that we are experiencing, we may speak too loudly (when excited); or we may speak so quietly that people cannot hear us or may observe that we are mumbling.

Let's think about the muscles involved in talking. If we are feeling tense as a result of the emotions we are experiencing, the muscles in our vocal tract will also be tense, resulting in shallow breathing, a tight throat, frequent swallowing or even the feeling of being 'tongue-tied'. Due to emotions such as fear and worry, muscle movements which are typically natural can feel unnatural or strange. If our communication skills are impacted by our emotions, we may subconsciously focus our attention on automatic body movements, such as how our tongue is moving when we speak. This unusual focus on an ordinarily automatic action can make it harder to move your tongue correctly and can therefore result in a challenge to clear articulation.

It is not just our muscle control which can be impacted by our emotions. Remember that at the start of the speech chain, we noted that listening is an essential skill for successful communication. If we are feeling overwhelmed by emotions, this can result in distracted thinking, making it more difficult to listen. This can affect communication, as the turn taking and responses required for fluent conversation will be impaired.

The speech chain also noted that for successful communication, we need to be able to access the right words and put them in the right order. There may have been times when you were so focused on saying the 'right thing', or thinking about what to say next or what you had just said, that this disrupted the flow of the conversation.

Emotions are physical feelings, they start in your body and arise out of your conscious control.

Mort 2021

We have considered the impact of our emotions physiologically on our speech process; but what the impact on our interactions with others?

Different emotions will evoke different physical reactions. Let's consider feelings of fear and worry. Our brains and bodies are programmed to scan the environment for threats. This is often an unconscious process, but one that was essential for the survival of the species. Humans are still programmed to do this; but for some individuals (both adults and children), this process can dominate. We must be aware that if we are experiencing these emotions, we may be unable to focus our attention on somebody trying to communicate with us. Our eye contact may be disrupted; our attention and listening skills may be impacted, meaning that we cannot focus on what somebody is saying to us or asking of us. These difficulties will impact on our ability to interact and communicate effectively.

Why do we need to know this and what does it mean for us in practice?

We have taken time to reflect on how our emotions can affect our communication skills as adults; so we must now consider the impact of emotions on children's communication skills. Children experience the same range of physiological changes that we do as adults; but they do not have the experience, knowledge or self-awareness to understand the impact of their emotions – and we must remember this.

 AN EDUCATOR'S EXPERIENCE...

We have worked with the brilliant Tythe Barn team, a pre-school setting in Gloucestershire. Cathy, one of the early years leads at the setting, shared this reflection:

In September 2021 we welcomed another cohort of children into Tythe Barn preschool following the Covid-19 pandemic. It became very apparent through observations, baseline assessments and discussions with parents/carers that lots of children found it extremely

*difficult to communicate their feelings and emotions. As profes-
sionals, we researched training opportunities and courses available
to support us in this area, and we came across Facts4Life. We were
approached to take part in a research project to develop children's
communication skills alongside their emotional development. This
was a fascinating project and we all gained and learned so many
new skills and strategies in supporting children in this area. We
have used the knowledge from the course to plan and deliver small
group sessions on a weekly basis to children who need this intervention. The results have been amazing and it is an area we will
most definitely continue to develop over the next academic year
and beyond.*

We have a responsibility to observe the situation and make an informed
decision about how to interact and communicate with a child who is overwhelmed by emotion. Remember that all children are unique and there is
no 'one size fits all' approach; but the physiological changes that occur in
the body when an individual is emotionally dysregulated means the child
may be unable to listen and follow instructions – so this is not the time to
make demands of them. If a child is overwhelmed by emotion, they may be
unable to find the right words to express themselves – so this is not the time
to ask them to talk about how they are feeling or ask lots of questions.

As Cathy's reflection shows us, we must observe how children are feeling and recognise when we need to extend our own knowledge and expertise – and, most importantly, how to use new information and resources to
make a positive difference to the children in our care.

FACTS4LIFE: REDEFINING HEALTH EDUCATION

Kelly Green, a curriculum developer at Facts4Life, summarises its
work here:

*Facts4Life is an approach to health education for all ages. It is the
brainchild of Dr Hugh van't Hoff, a practising GP, who collabo-
rated with a group of teachers to develop training and resources*

to help empower children and their families on matters relating to their health and wellbeing.

The approach seeks to build health resilience and to challenge commonly held beliefs about how we experience health. Central to this is the exploration of three key messages:

- **Riding the ups and downs:** Sometimes we feel well, sometimes not. That's normal.
- **Keeping balanced:** We often don't recognise that most of the time, most of us get better from most illnesses without medical help.
- **Smoothing the path:** We can learn to take greater responsibility for our health and respond positively to life's challenges.

All of our resources are built on these three key messages in a spiral curriculum that seeks to give children and young people a common language to better understand and communicate issues relating to their experience of health and illness.

Our work initially began in primary schools in Gloucestershire, but soon developed to include the secondary stage and then early years. We recognised how important it is to communicate these key messages from a young age and to widen the reach to embrace families in developing healthy attitudes, understanding and behaviour.

We live in a climate where many worry about health and we often assume that perfect health is attainable. These unrealistic expectations can lead to the idea that medical services should be able to step in and fix us whenever we feel unwell.

We believe that by developing a language to talk about our experience of health and illness, we can take greater ownership of the factors that affect us. Our work has been independently evaluated by the University of the West of England, and has shown that by building our understanding, we can develop positive attitudes and change behaviour.

The Covid-19 pandemic brought the issues of health and illness into sharp focus in the public consciousness. Never has there been a better time for people to reflect on how they can positively shape their relationship with their own health and wellbeing. This is further amplified *by the current strain on the National Health Service and the growing conversation about our nation's need to reduce demand on services by adopting more preventative behaviours. This isn't black and white – people are complex beings and rarely do we engage in unhealthy behaviours for the reasons we shouldn't. This is why mental health and its relationship to how we feel in our bodies feature so prominently in the Facts4Life approach; and why our suite of training opportunities on this theme has been so popular across settings for all ages.*

We are thrilled to see projects such as Facts4Life working with early years teams and children. These first years are so important for early experiences and brain development, and children need us to work with them to understand their emotions and find strategies that will support emotional wellbeing going forward.

It is so important that we build emotional vocabulary with children. We can provide the language which describes the big feelings they are experiencing and then give them a platform to explore those needs and feelings.

It is important to use the correct terms for such emotions while describing the impact on the brain and body, so that from the youngest age, children can develop the competence to identify them and receive the co-regulation they need to reach a state of calm.

Conkbayir 2023

Remember this question…

What percentage of critical brain development happens in the first five years of life?

1. 50%
2. 70%
3. 90%

Answer: 90%. What an important role we have in early years!

Summary

Humans are social beings and feeling safe is very high on our agenda. If we do not feel safe, we are constantly scanning our surroundings looking for threats. This takes a huge amount of energy and if we are busy scanning our environment for danger, we cannot focus and learn, which in turn may impact on development.

We have a really important role in showing children that they are safe and that they matter to us. By doing this through the connections we make, we can enable children to access their learning environment, to develop their sense of self and to reach their potential.

 ## Further reading and research ideas

Debbie Garvey (2023). *Little Brains Matter: A Practical Guide to Brain Development and Neuroscience in Early Childhood.* Routledge.

Facts4Life
www.facts4life.org

Hayley Rice - child and adolescent psychotherapist
www.hayley-rice.com

Kinder Education
www.facebook.com/Kindereducation/

Dr Lala Manners (2019). *The Early Years Movement Handbook: A Principles-Based Approach to Supporting Young Children's Physical Development, Health and Wellbeing.* Jessica Kingsley Publishers.

Dr Mine Conkabyir (2022). *The Neuroscience of the Developing Child: Self-Regulation for Wellbeing and a Sustainable Future*. Routledge.

Suzanne Zeedyk (2020). *Sabre Tooth Tigers & Teddy Bears: The Connected Baby Guide to Understanding Attachment*. Connected Baby.

Speech, language and communication needs

Many children experience various different types of difficulties in communicating.

'Speech, language and communication needs' (SLCN) is an umbrella term that refers to difficulties with one or multiple aspects of communication. These can include difficulties:

- Understanding what others are saying (language comprehension).
- Formulating sentences (expressive language).
- Saying sounds and words (speech).
- Speaking fluently (stammering).
- Using language socially (social communication).
- Speaking in front of people (selective mutism).

What might these difficulties look like and what strategies can you use to support the child?

Understanding what others say:

- The child watches and copies other children.
- The child does not follow brief instructions.
- The child does not become engaged in activities with a high language content.
- The child is asked to do things lots of times, but doesn't respond.
- The child is regularly last to follow instructions.

DOI: 10.4324/9781003335429-4

- The child does not play with toys in the usual way or in a similar way to their peers.
- The child becomes upset/frustrated when they have not understood what to do.
- The child echoes the language of adults (echolalia).

Strategies to support:

- Speak slowly and clearly.
- Reduce your language – use fewer words in sentences and stress the most important words (eg, 'Max, get your coat').
- Repeat, repeat, repeat! This is how children learn vocabulary.
- Use the child's name to gain their attention. Ensure that they are looking at you when you speak.
- Use visual clues – real objects (objects of reference), photographs and pictures (symbols) – to help the child understand what is happening next (eg, 'Snack time', 'Tidy up time', 'Home time').
- Comment on what the child is doing – give them words that reflect what's happening (eg, 'You're building'; 'That's a house').
- Follow the child's lead – join them in an activity they are engaged in and comment on their play. Have fun as you play together.

Formulating sentences:

- The child takes you to things they want, but may not yet have the words to refer to them.
- The child mainly points/grunts.
- You find it difficult to work out what the child means/wants.
- The child gets frustrated/upset at not being able to get their message across.
- The child uses 'babytalk' (eg, 'choo-choo' instead of 'train').
- The child only uses single words, not sentences.
- The child does not use a range of words (vocabulary) (eg, all animals are 'dogs'; all people are 'mummy').
- The child asks the same question lots of times.

- The child repeats all or part of what an adult has said.
- The child doesn't appear to want to communicate.

Strategies to support:

- Give them a reason to communicate – consider putting some toys slightly out of reach to increase the need for the child to communicate to play with them.
- Offer choices – for example, at snack time, 'Milk or water?'
- Be a good role model – speak slowly and clearly; and don't ask the child to repeat your words.
- Give them time to respond – when you talk to the child, speak and then pause for a little longer to give the child extra time to respond (remember the speech chain).
- Consider the different ways in which the child can tell you what they want – for example:
  - Saying what they want.
  - Responding to your offer of a choice between two things.
  - Pointing to what they want (you can help by then saying the word).
  - Choosing from one of two pictures or symbols – the child can point and you can then say the word.
- Make encouraging sound and noises (eg, symbolic noises for animals/vehicles).
- Repeat words.
- Be a good language role model – extend the child's utterance (eg, they say, 'Ball'; you say, 'Throw the ball').
- Avoid guessing what the child might be requesting – for example, 'Evie always has milk, so I'll give her milk.' Give them the chance to make a choice.
- Reduce questions. To encourage the child to give you information, try starting a sentence and see if the child can fill in the gap (eg, 'Look what's in the bag – it's a ...').

Saying sounds and words:

- Adults find it difficult to understand the child's speech.

- The child misses the beginning or end of words (eg, 'cat' becomes '-at'; 'bus' becomes 'bu-').
- The child mixes up sounds or has difficulty with specific sounds.
- The child is a messy eater, drools excessively or has difficulty sucking through a straw.

Strategies to support:

- Support parents with dummy/bottle use. Overuse of a dummy and/or bottle can result in speech and language difficulties. We advise that dummy use stop when the baby starts babbling (typically around six months), so that they do not speak with the dummy in their mouth, leading to incorrect speech patterns. If the baby needs the dummy in order to settle to sleep, this is important; but parents should ensure that the child does not have the dummy in their mouth when they are awake and babbling/talking.
- Check hearing – hearing and speech go hand in hand, so parents may want to talk to their health visitor about a hearing test.
- Draw attention to everyday noises to begin to fine-tune listening skills.
- Explore noise makers – play 'Guess which one?' The child listens with their eyes closed, to see if they can find the noise maker.
- Make funny faces in the mirror – kissing shapes; smiling shapes; sticking your tongue out or moving it side to side.
- If you are aware of the sounds the child finds difficult, be a good sound role model – for example, use sound bags, songs and stories.
- Don't correct the child – repeat their message slowly to show you have heard and to serve as a good sound role model.

Fluency:

- The child's speech sounds 'bumpy' – they repeat whole words or parts of words.
- The child's speech appears very effortful and they struggle to get words out.
- The child may go red in the face, as if they are holding their breath.

Strategies to support:

- Give the child time to finish and do not finish their words for them.
- Listen attentively – show the child you are interested in what they are saying, not how they say it.
- Use the child's name frequently to reinforce their sense of identity as someone who is special to you.
- Maintain normal eye contact and show the child that they have your attention. Frequent nodding, or getting on with another task while they speak, may make the child feel rushed.
- Ensure that your body language is relaxed and open, as non-verbal communication conveys important messages to the speaker about the attention and interest of the listener.
- Slow down your own speech, adding natural pauses, to show the child that there is no need to rush.
- Allow the child to make one-word answers if they are obviously struggling to speak. They also may enjoy speaking with another child by saying a rhyme or similar.
- If the child is struggling to speak, acknowledge the effort they are making with a kind comment (eg, 'You did really well there to say that word').

(Adapted from the British Stammering Association – www.stamma.org.)

Social communication:

- The child does not make eye contact during interaction.
- The child tends to play alone.
- The child uses little or no language.
- The child has a poor understanding or use of body language.
- The child misinterprets or fails to pick up on 'clues' for understanding social situations.

- The child learns a set of behaviours in one situation but has difficulty transferring those skills to other situations.

Strategies to support:

- What does the child enjoy? Can you include another child/adult in their game?
- Support the child in doing simple tasks involving other children (eg, handing out plates at snack time).
- Introduce simple turn-taking games between you and the child. Taking turns is a vital element of shared play. Talk about what's happening (eg, 'Rebecca's turn … Harry's turn').
- Encourage people games – in people games, children aren't distracted by toys. They focus on the adult. The back-and-forth nature of people games is similar to that of a conversation, only with fewer words.

Selective mutism:

- The child may speak fluently in some situations but remain consistently silent in others.
- The child may have a blank expression or appear 'frozen' when expected to speak.

Strategies to support:

- Have patience and let the child speak when they are ready.
- Engage the child through physical activity and/or creative activities.
- Talk to the child about what you are doing without expecting an answer.
- Provide the opportunity to speak (eg, 'I wonder where this one goes …?' [Pause]).
- Organise activities in which the child can talk, sing and move in unison; and activities/games which do not require speech.

- Do NOT make it your mission to get the child to talk.
- Do NOT make the child say 'please/thank you' – they are not being rude.
- Do NOT react when the child finally talks.

(Adapted from the Selective Mutism Information and Research Association – www.smira.org.)

Developmental language disorder

Developmental language disorder (DLD) is a diagnosis given by a speech and language therapist to people who have lifelong difficulties with talking and understanding words. These difficulties create barriers to communication and learning in everyday life, and aren't due to another condition (Speech and Language UK).

It is estimated that two children in every class of 30 have DLD. The difficulties that result can impact on other areas of learning, on friendships and on mental health.

Working collaboratively with speech and language therapists is essential in order to support children with SLCN.

Here is how to get the most out of speech and language therapy support:

- Work collaboratively – different roles bring out different knowledge and perspectives when supporting children. Use these strengths to work together.
- Work with the child and their family when planning support and targets. Really listen to the child and their family, which will make the support meaningful and relevant. What are the child and their family's aspirations?
- Request support at key times – for example, transition into school.
- Re-refer if you are concerned or if new concerns arise.
- Request time with the speech therapist if possible to observe how they work with the child and ask them to demonstrate strategies/ recommendations.

Are the children in your setting truly 'heard'? How can we enable the voice of the child?

'The voice of the child' is a term that is often heard in the early years sector; but do we really stop and think about what this means in practice – and, most importantly, what it means for the child?

'The voice of the child' refers to what children say directly; but it also refers to many other aspects of their communication: their behaviour, their choices in play and interaction, what and when they choose to eat – the list goes on. It is important that when we are thinking about the voice of the child, we really try to 'hear and see' what the child is experiencing from their point of view. This is important when communicating with all children; but we must be aware that when a child has an SLCN, it is even more important that we take the time to 'hear' them.

Children with SLCN may express themselves in ways that are not easily understood by others. Remember that all behaviour is communication. Our role is to 'know' the children –to learn how they communicate and understand how we need to communicate with them in order for them to access their learning environment and make sense of their world. Being in a situation where you don't understand what is being said to you or can't express yourself in a way that can be understood by others can be a scary and isolating experience. We have a duty of care to ensure that all children understand and are understood, however they communicate.

Why is it important to 'hear' the voice of the child?

Children have the right to have their opinions heard and their views respected in decision-making that affects them.

Article 12 of the United Nations Convention on the Rights of the Child (1989)

When another person knows us, they take the time to really listen to us, our thoughts and opinions; they respect us even if they would approach a situation differently from us; they enjoy our company and share interests. This all makes us feel valued and supported, which in turn enables us to feel safe and secure.

When a child feels safe and secure in their early years environment, they will feel more able to be themselves; to approach their play and learning in a way that matters to them; and to approach and experience the world in a more confident way. We can promote self-esteem and self-worth when we value and enable the voice of the child. In order for a child to develop their play, to explore and actively learn, and to develop key critical thinking skills, they will need to feel confident in their environment and secure in the knowledge that their voice and who they are will be heard, seen and respected.

MINDFUL MOMENT...

When we are truly listened to by another person, how do we feel? When you are talking about something important to you and the listener shows real interest by asking relevant questions and wanting to know more about your experience, how does this make you feel?

This process of active listening is so important for children. When children are truly 'heard', they will feel important, and that what they have to say or communicate is significant. This will then strengthen the relationship and bond between you.

When we 'hear' and 'see' children, we are supporting them in developing a sense of belonging and building the confidence to express their thoughts and opinions – an important skill for the future.

In summary, our role in early years is to create meaningful engagement with children. We need to understand **all** children and give them the opportunity to express themselves; but we must be mindful of the critical difference this can make to children with SLCN.

This is not easy, as we can't ever really know what a person is thinking; but when a child can tell us what they are thinking, this really helps us to understand them. We must acknowledge that it is more challenging to understand and 'hear' a child if they do not yet have words, or if their speech is disordered and very difficult to understand.

How do we do this?

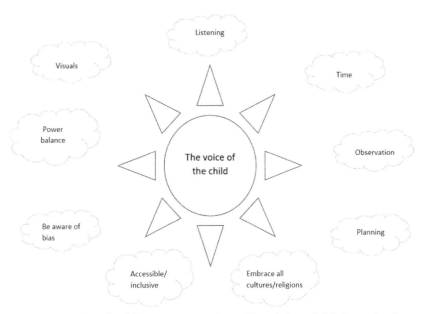

We need to build a picture and profile of the child through direct engagement, observations and conversations with parents/carers and the wider family/community.

Listening

We have already touched on the importance of 'active listening'; but how do we do this in a busy early years environment?

MINDFUL MOMENT...

Think about a time when you were talking and the other person was clearly distracted. They may have looked at a message on their smart watch or started talking about something completely different.

How did you feel? Did you feel valued? Did you feel that the other person was interested in you and what you were telling them?

How did you then respond? Did you go back to what you wanted to say originally? Did you tell them that you had something you wanted to say? Did you address the fact that they weren't listening to you?

This can be a tricky situation to manage socially and we need to be aware of how we listen and engage in conversation. Are we good at listening and turn taking; or do we tend to take over and finish the other person's sentences? Do we make the conversation about 'us' when the other person wants to talk about something that has happened to them?

Please reflect honestly on your own listening skills, as these are essential for successful communication and interaction.

We can listen during children's play. When you listen actively, you will hear the child's imagination evolving, and understand how they interact with their peers and how this may change depending on who they are playing with, and where and what they are playing.

Listen to the conversations that children have with each other; and try not to jump in and change them with your own thoughts and ideas. There will also be opportunities to listen to and observe the conversations that children have with the adults in the setting, as well as with their family members – how do they interact, initiate and respond?

Taking the time to actively listen will enable you to hear children's ideas and observe their opinions grow. What a brilliant way to start to truly understand the child's experiences from their own point of view!

If you are struggling to understand what a child is telling you due to their speech difficulties, you can acknowledge this challenge. Phrases such as, 'I'm sorry – my ears didn't hear that properly,' 'I didn't hear that – can you show me?' and 'Learning to talk can be tricky' are useful, as we are recognising the 'breakdown' in communication but are putting the focus on us and on our listening, rather than on the child's speech sound difficulty.

Don't ask children to repeat words back to us or ask them to say a word 'correctly' – they would do this already if they could. Just model back phrases so that the child can hear the correct pronunciation – this also shows the child that you are interested and confirms that you have understood them. Many children know when we are pretending to understand, which makes us look insincere and uninterested, potentially affecting the child's self-esteem and confidence to communicate. Be honest and work together to see whether you can 'repair' the communication breakdown.

Top tips to show that you are actively listening include the following:

- Use your body language. Some children may not be comfortable with eye contact, so be mindful of this and just turn your body towards the child, respecting their space at all times.
- Watch and observe the child's facial expressions and body language – this is important for all children, but especially for children with SLCN, as it will provide you with some clues as to what they may be trying to communicate to you.
- It can be tempting to ask lots of questions when a child is telling us something, as we often want to keep the conversation going; but in fact this can stall conversation. It can be more useful to use prompts such as, 'Tell me more about ...' This shows the child that you are interested in what they are telling you, but you are not directing the conversation.
- Allow the child to speak freely – try not to finish their sentences or jump in with your own thoughts and ideas, as this can alter what the child was planning to tell you and may divert them away from sharing something that really matters to them.
- Don't rush to problem solve – sometimes children just want to tell us about something that has happened or how they are feeling, rather than wanting us to do something about it. We can listen and support by commenting on how they are feeling – 'You seem really sad about that.'

Time

When a child speaks to us, we must give them time to speak freely. We can reflect on what they are saying to us and ask questions to gain more information if appropriate (but always remember to be careful with questions). It is so important that we listen to the child's ideas and opinions without judgement. By allowing the child to speak freely, we are showing them that we value who they are and what they have to say.

Children who do not feel valued, supported or listened to may feel less able to share their thoughts and opinions, so it is so important that when a child speaks to us, we stop what we are doing and listen carefully to what they are telling us. When we stop and turn our body towards the child, making eye contact if the child is comfortable with that, we are showing them that we are interested in what they have to say – we are listening and engaging with them. If we are already engaged with another child and cannot move our focus to the child who is seeking our time, we must acknowledge this: 'I am just talking to Jack – when we finish, I will be able to listen to you.' Remember that you must always then act on this and find the child once you are in a position to give them your full attention.

Observation

We know that observation is such an important skill to develop in the early years environment. It is essential if we are to understand each unique child and how they approach the world. When we observe children in our settings, we can tune into each child's likes and dislikes, and their stage of development. It can be helpful to add a section on your observation record sheets for the 'child's voice', which can serve as a reminder to keep this at the forefront of your observations.

Planning

When you observe and pay particular attention to the child's voice, you can then use this information to inform your planning. You could include a section on your planning sheet to take into account the child's voice, commenting on their interests and recording your observations. Remember that children with SLCN may be at risk of not being 'heard', so it is vital to include these children in planning ideas. Look for patterns of play that you might not understand. Some children may play in ways that don't make sense to us, but we must trust that the child is exploring play in a way that is meaningful to them. We need to respect this and identify how we can plan to extend the child's play patterns and ideas further.

Embrace all cultures/religions

Develop your knowledge in this area by speaking to the child and their family about their culture and religion. When you celebrate all cultures and religions, you are showing the child that they are valued and encouraging them to express their feelings and thoughts about what they believe in and who they are as a person.

Accessible and inclusive environment

Having well-resourced and accessible areas gives children choice and enables them to express their interest and have a voice. It is easy to remember the phrase, 'Offer choice, enable a voice' – this is especially important for children with SLCN.

Be aware of your own bias

We all have our own preferences for where we want to be (eg, inside/outside), what we play with and how we play with it. We must be able to reflect on our own bias, so that we don't react negatively to children who have different preferences; but we can still use these opportunities as teaching moments. For example, we can say it's okay not to like playing outdoors, but can explain to children why exercise and fresh air are good for us.

MINDFUL MOMENT...

Where do you feel you do your best teaching? Do you feel happier when you are outside with the children or do you prefer being snuggled up in the book corner?

Take a moment to think about where you like to be in the early years environment. Educators feel more comfortable, motivated and engaged when they are working in their preferred area.

If you work in a team, talk about this together and support each other in knowing your own preferences and potential biases. You can then work in a way that makes the most of every educator's strengths. All children will benefit from this self-reflection.

Empower the child

Adults do hold all the power, so it is important to be aware of this and empower children to make decisions about their day where possible. By enabling children to make their own decisions, we are giving them a voice. This decision making can be as simple as choosing which story they would like to read or what to have for a snack. We've said it already – 'Offer choice, enable a voice.'

If you choose to do circle time in your setting, you can invite the children to decide what they want to talk about – they can express themselves and create their own conversations. Remember the children with SLCN – how can they be included? How do you need to adapt your circle time so that all children can express themselves and understand what is happening?

Use visuals

Symbols and pictures cards can be used to support choice making. You could present the cards to the child at the beginning of the session so that they can control their own play choices; or they can be used at more structured times, such as snack time or when singing songs. Offering visuals enables children to have a voice when they don't have the language skills to express themselves verbally.

Some children may use signs, such as Makaton, to communicate. Think about your setting – how inclusive is it? If you are using signs to support communication, do all the adults sign? Are we signing 'please' and 'thank you' to teach good manners; or are we using signs which are functional and will be useful for the child with SLCN in order to get their needs met? When using signs, think about the individual child and what words will be most useful/important to them. We need vocabulary to be both functional and relevant to that child, their family and their story.

MINDFUL MOMENT...

Take a moment to reflect: how do you 'hear' your children in your setting? How do you capture the voice of the child and how do you use this information in your planning and environment?

What can hinder communication development and what can support it?

There are multiple theories on language development; but it is generally agreed that the early years are a critical period for this development, and that these skills underpin so many other areas of children's development. The development of communication skills is vital for learning, making relationships, having autonomy and becoming independent.

We have talked a lot about listening to the voice of the child and why this matters;

so we must also acknowledge that if we do not actively listen to each child's voice, the child may feel that we do not value their perspective and thus that we do not value them.

> *Disregard for children's voices diminishes their experiences of autonomy and self-regulation which in turn reduced their motivation to learn.*
>
> Murray 2019

As an adult, if you are engaged in a conversation with another person and they are clearly not listening to you and not showing interest, how do you react? It is possible that you may stop talking or perhaps change the conversation. When we do not actively listen to children, they may lose the motivation to talk to us. The quality of the adult-child interaction is crucial for supporting communication development; and if we are not engaged fully with a child, we may be hindering their opportunity to build on their speech and language skills.

So, how can we support communication development?

- Be a 'tuned-in' adult.
- Ensure quality interactions.
- Engage in active listening.
- Look for patterns of play.
- Know how the child communicates.
- Reflect on your communication and interaction style.

An interesting study by Romeo et al (2018) concluded that it is the quality of the communication exchange between adult and child which has the biggest positive impact on language growth for the child, rather than just the amount of language that the child is exposed to.

The researchers used child-worn language recorders and brain imaging to study brain activity during communication. Their findings showed increased activation in the frontal lobe and increased Broca's area activation (the part of the brain involved in language expression) when children and adults engaged in back-and-forth 'conversation'.

This highlights the importance of 'tuning in' to the children we are with. We must follow their lead in play; and we must listen carefully and observe all their communication so that we can respond sensitively and add to this communication exchange. If we relate this to what the researchers have summarised, we can see that when we are a 'tuned-in' adult, we are helping the child's brain to grow!

What is the long-term impact of SLCN on mental health/emotional wellbeing? What are the risks to the child if we don't support SLCN in the early years?

Across the UK, for 1.7 million children learning to talk and understand words feels like an impossible hurdle – this increases to one in four for those children living in disadvantaged areas of the UK.

Speechandlanguage.org.uk

It is estimated that 10% of all children have SLCN which may be complex and long term; while around 50% of children on school entry have more transient difficulties but, with the right level of support, will make good progress with their speech and language skills (Law et al 2020).

There is a correlation between children with SLCN and:

- Low achievement.
- Behavioural and emotional difficulties – 81% of children with emotional and behavioural disorders have significant language difficulties (Hollo et al 2014).
- Mental health challenges.
- Poor employment.
- Youth crime.

Children with language difficulties are at greater risk of behavioural, social and emotional difficulties in childhood and through adolescence (Lindsay & Dockrell 2012).

This does not mean that the future is pre-determined for all children with SLCN; but what we do know is that we must provide the right support for these children as soon as possible to enable them to access their social and learning environments and to achieve their potential.

Due to their limited conversation skills, poor non-verbal skills and limited social understanding, children with SLCN are at greater risk of rejection and isolation, as they struggle with peer interaction and with forming meaningful friendships (speechandlanguage.org.uk).

This social isolation can result in lower self-esteem and have a significant impact on emotional wellbeing.

Take a moment to read and process the following statistic: 66% to 90% of young offenders have low language skills, with 46% to 67% of these being in the poor or very poor range (Bryan et al 2007).

For further reading in this area, visit the website of the Royal College of Speech and Language Therapists, where you can access some interesting articles (www.rcslt.org).

We do know that SLCN can be a major barrier to accessing the curriculum and to developing and maintaining relationships. At the start of this book, we discussed why we communicate and what it means to us as humans to be able to communicate. If young person finds themselves unable to access their 'community' because of SLCN, this can have a major impact on their wellbeing, which is worrying.

Communicating with children with SLCN – how can we adapt our own interaction to help the child to feel valued, confident and understood?

 AN EDUCATOR'S EXPERIENCE...

Please take some time to read and reflect on this powerful case study shared with us by a colleague who has had roles both in early years and most recently in a mainstream school as a one-to-one teaching assistant:

This child has a diagnosis of autism spectrum condition. She is generally non-verbal and communicates largely by leading an adult to what she wants or where she wants to go. She doesn't make eye contact and is unable to use expressive language. When I first met the child, she had seen many teaching assistants (TAs) come and go, and I was told that she cried all day and was generally unsettled. In order to improve her situation and make her feel understood, I applied the following strategies.

In order to create a bond with her, I spent the first week observing her and getting to know her interests, her schema, her non-verbal ways of communicating, her family and what made her feel happy and safe. I noticed that she babbled to herself a lot while playing, and that her schema was transporting. She loved walking around the school and carrying her lunch bag and other items around. Sometimes I would offer to carry the items myself. I had also learned from the class teacher that her family was interested in music, so we spent a few minutes every afternoon playing a few songs on the piano. She would get excited and run around in circles behind me while I played; and she would run over and put my hands back on the keys to continue playing if she wasn't ready for me to stop. She eventually had a go; and when she did, she could play Twinkle, Twinkle *all the way through, having learned it by ear!*

I generally followed her lead and went where she wanted to go, almost as though she was showing me her world. I mimicked some of her movements as she played – for example, looking at toys closely and from different angles. She would later start handing me toys to play with exactly as she did: looking at them, pretending to measure them and babbling, before lining them up next to each other. She had a timetable with 15-minute intervals, which I arranged with the class teacher to make it a bit more relaxed and flexible – mostly to allow her time to finish her play. I was always calm and tuned in to what her needs were, sometimes anticipating that she was about to tire herself out after spending too much time on one activity. I would distract her by offering to go for a walk or to the nurture room, where she loved to relax sitting on beanbags.

It was important to create opportunities for communication. One of the most useful strategies I utilised was pausing and giving her time to think and respond in the best way she could. For example, I would pause when singing a song halfway through, which would result in her turning to look at my mouth for a second or two, sometimes reaching for my mouth to 'ask' me to continue. On other occasions, I would sing two of her favourite songs – Roly Poly *and* Wind the Bobbin Up *– and then I would pause and ask her which one to sing next. She would blurt out in response, 'Roly Poly!', while grabbing my hands to continue the song. This strategy continues to work and I have used it in phonics and maths – for example, counting to 19 and waiting for her to shout '20!' Other times, I would pretend to not know what shape she wanted me to make next using playdough. It's an activity she loves, so it's a great opportunity to take turns and get her to try to communicate what she wants. For example, I would draw a few shapes (which she likes drawn in a particular order and in particular colours), and then I would pretend I didn't know which shape to draw next. She would take my hand and place it on the page in frustration; and eventually she would blurt it out or turn the page to the shape she wanted next. Other times, I would give her a choice or give her things bit by bit, so she could ask for them either by making eye contact or verbally.*

Employing singing and constant chatter as a strategy not only gives her the vocabulary, but also model the situations and contexts in which the vocabulary is used. For example, if she was playing with kitchen toys, I would sit by her and pretend to cook a meal, list out the ingredients and use vocabulary such as 'stirring' and 'simmering'. I noticed instantly that the child loves singing and babbling to herself. Sometimes I would mimic the sounds she was making, which would create some sort of back-and-forth and would make her giggle and make eye contact. I would also mimic her movements while sitting next to her and playing alongside her.

After working with this child for some time, I have noticed great improvements in her communication. Having the consistency of the same TA every day and building a close relationship have caused her to become much more settled and happier. She is much calmer and is more vocal and bubbly – evidence that she now feels safe. From being completely non-verbal, she now says a few words and sentences; her vocabulary has increased greatly and she can say words in context. She also recalls and repeats words and phrases used by the TA, such as, 'It's nice to see you' and lines from songs or other language that she has heard. She also responds to her name and sometimes she will look at something that the TA is pointing at. She has started making brief eye contact with the TA and can follow some instructions, such as, 'Sit nicely'; and it is clear that she understands her daily routines. She has been pointing at books and diagrams to indicate her preferences, and has used words/sounds to communicate what activity she wants to do, such as naming a shape that she wants or sounding out a letter she wants to write. I believe that this growth in communication in response to the strategies shows that she feels heard; that she has a good emotional relationship with her TA; and on the whole, that she feels understood. She is no longer crying to communicate her needs and is a happy child, seldom frustrated.

This is a brilliant example of an educator taking the time to 'know' a child and finding ways to change how they were interacting and teaching, rather than expecting the child to change. The result of this approach is that the child feels valued, respected and understood – which, as we know, is the foundation they need to be able to learn.

Reflecting on our own communication and interaction styles

We all have our own individual communication and interaction styles because we are *unique*.

> ## MINDFUL MOMENT...
>
> - What sort of language do we use when talking to our closest friends? What is the pace of the conversation like?
> - How do we communicate with work colleagues? Do we use the same style of communication? Perhaps with our peers; but what about when talking to a management team or to an Ofsted inspector?
> - Do we alter our communication and interaction style when talking to an elderly friend or relative?
>
> It is likely that the answer to most of these reflective question is 'yes'. Generally, we will alter our communication style to meet the needs of the person we are talking to; this is a hugely positive attribute to have.

Let's consider our own communication and interaction skills as educators. Talking to children requires a high level of skill that we might not have considered. As we know, all children develop their communication and interaction skills at different rates. Some children need a high level of adult support in order to be understood; whereas others can engage in a two-way conversation from the age of two! This variation demands that the adults working with these children be able to adapt and communicate with a child whether they are verbal or non-verbal.

MINDFUL MOMENT...

Time for some honest reflection: read the following descriptors – do any resonate with you?

- **The 'rigid routiner':** Routine is important to this adult. They find change difficult and having clear structure to the day makes them feel secure. They like to plan and set up activities so that they can feel in control of the session. The 'rigid routiner' is so focused on staying on schedule that this results in limited interaction with the children.
- **The 'party practitioner':** This adult is all-singing, all-dancing! They are fun, but they don't always notice how the children are feeling, as they are doing most of the playing and the talking. As a result, the children have fewer opportunities to take an active role in the interaction.
- **The 'disengaged educator':** This adult appears to be a bit of a bystander. They are with the children, but are quiet and don't always notice or respond when a child initiates an interaction. As a result, the child may feel that they don't matter to this adult and are not important, and that what they have to say or share with others is not valued.
- **The 'adulterating adult':** This adult leads the play and may change how the child is playing, as they have their own ideas about play. They often 'help' a child to do something before the child has expressed the need for help and they may ask many questions. As a result, the child may feel disempowered: they are not enabled to follow their own patterns of play and therefore are not play-ing in a way that is meaningful to them. When the adult does most of the talking and asks lots of questions, the child has fewer opportunities to speak and share their ideas, resulting in feelings of frustration, disengagement and unimportance.
- **The 'connection creator':** This adult is aware of children's feelings and emotions. They validate the child's feelings and understand the importance of play, following and extending the child's ideas.

This communication and interaction style helps the child to have autonomy and know that they are valued. The child has regular and consistent opportunities to initiate interaction, either verbally or non-verbally, and the adult responds sensitively.

You may recognise elements of your communication and interaction style in each of those descriptors; but the key message here is to reflect. It may also be helpful to support each other through peer observation. Every child is unique, so you will need to adapt your communication and interaction skills accordingly. We must acknowledge that how we communicate and interact will impact on how a child feels and how they themselves learn to communicate and interact.

There will be times when an adult's communication and interaction style do not match and support a child's style, which can result in the adult and child not 'connecting'. This can feel frustrating and ultimately can lead to the child not accessing quality opportunities for language learning.

MINDFUL MOMENT...

Take a moment to think about the children in your setting:

- Which children do you really enjoy interacting with?
- Which children do you spend less time with?
- How do these children communicate and interact?

This reflection is important, as it will help you to explore whether you are spending less time or communicating less with children who are quieter or who aren't yet speaking. We need to identify this so that we can do something about it.

In an interesting Australian study by Torr et al (2016), the research team explored language used by early years practitioners and found that the adults tended to talk to more than one child at a time, limiting their potential to engage in the types of sustained conversations with individual children that have been shown to promote language development. The study also revealed that the adults' language was used primarily to manage behaviour and for routine care (eg, toileting, handwashing), rather than to support conversation around the children's play and experiences. This suggests that there are still many missed opportunities for developing natural conversation skills and sharing play and interests.

We are aware from our conversations with early years educators that supporting children with SLCN in the early years environment can be challenging, for many different reasons. It is important that we reflect honestly about these challenges so that we can support each other and share ideas.

AN EDUCATOR'S EXPERIENCE...

Nicola Cooper, an early years educator and special educational needs coordinator (SENDCO), shares her experiences with us:

I've worked in early years for seven years and for five of those I've had the pleasure of being an early years SENDCO. Over the last five years, I have seen a significant shift in the type of support we are providing in our setting, with the emphasis now being on SLCN. We've always had children who need that additional support if their language skills are a little delayed – providing small group games, additional time with their key person, focused sound activities etc; but what we are witnessing now is quite different. Post-COVID, we are seeing a huge rise in the number of children entering our setting between the ages of two and three who simply lack social communication skills, listening and attention skills, and don't have language development appropriate to their age. Thus, we see a lot more frustration in the children who just can't make their needs understood, leading to friction with their peers.

Prior to COVID, it was easy enough to make a referral to the speech and language team and feel confident that those children referred would be seen. I'd then receive some great advice and ideas to work through, as would the child's parents; and we'd feel like progress was being made. Post-COVID, speech and lan-guage therapists are like a mirage in a never-ending desert of children with additional needs. I know they are there and they are striving to provide the great service they always have; but the waiting lists are long, initial consultations with parents and children are now being carried out on Zoom and we hadn't seen one in our setting for many a moon until very recently. I feel like we're (early years) becoming more and more confident in our own ability to provide our children with speech and lan-guage strategies and outcomes to work towards, as we've had to be resourceful while waiting for professional input; or we're going back to previous reports and using ideas from those – or good old Google!

With the increasing number of children who need additional support, we've moved to a total communication outlook for our children – with support and training from the Gloucestershire Early Years Team – in the hope that this will benefit all our chil-dren. Embedding this approach fully is taking time, as some staff find it harder and less natural than others to use Makaton or vis-ual aids, for example. I think improvement is expected instantly, when with many of our current children we are in it for the long haul. They need consistency, repetition, staff that listen to them, an environment that makes communication natural and easy, and parents who are on board to support them too.

Next to the long wait for professional support, our other biggest challenge is parents. We spend a lot of time sharing ideas, tips, resources and strategies with parents, but they are very seldom used. Even when therapists are involved and we've got a clear report with concise outcomes to work towards, it often feels like we are alone in putting these in place for the child. It can be a frus-trating job; but on those occasions when your hard work pays off and the child that you've been using Makaton and modelling lan-guage with for eight weeks or more just to communicate that they want their lunch box open, then says 'Open,' it's all worthwhile and it keeps you going!

What do children with SLCN need from us?

Communication respect is key!

Many settings adopt a total communication approach to ensure that all forms of communication are valued and respected, including signing, use of visuals and other low-tech communication systems. This is not an easy approach, but training courses are available so that teams can develop their knowledge and skills in this area and develop their understanding of different ways to communicate.

Children with communication difficulties need us to know what their communication method is. We can learn this through our observations; through liaising with other professionals such as speech and language therapists; and, most importantly, through conversation with the child's family. How does the child communicate their needs in their home environment and with the people who are closest to them?

Communication is a shared responsibility: we must ensure that the environment supports the child in communicating regardless of the level of their communication skills. Consider the noise level and any distractions that can be reduced to make it easier for the child to process information and express themselves. Keep your language clear and simple; and always ensure that you have the child's attention before communicating with them – they need to know that you are talking to them specifically.

Listen and look carefully at what the child is trying to communicate to you; and remember to give them time and space to express themselves, whether verbally or non-verbally.

It may sound obvious, but we must always treat children with SLCN with dignity and respect (as we should any child). There are many occasions when conversations about a child's needs and difficulties are had literally above their heads – sometimes between colleagues, but also when a professional comes to observe the child in the setting. This is not respectful; we must have professional conversations about children away from them, in a private and confidential setting.

CASE STUDY

A mum to a little girl born with a cleft lip and palate and hearing difficulties shared her experiences with us:

Q: How do your daughter's communication difficulties impact on her?

- At nursery, she didn't make great relationships with her peers as they didn't sign.
- Peers at school forget and misread her as being rude/ignoring them.
- She wants to be like everyone else.
- She is aware of being different.
- She can worry about upcoming appointments and operations.
- She's not getting any help; she's so well behaved, school says there's nothing wrong.
- She struggles with tiredness and going to school – I think it's overwhelming for her.
- She is very sensitive and attached to me. Nursery were aware of this and were very in tune with this; however, it has been a shock how this has not continued into her primary setting.

Q: How has this impacted on you as a family?

- I've blamed myself for something I did/didn't do during pregnancy.
- It's put a huge strain on all.
- I wish we could take it away from her.
- I've had to learn Makaton, then British Sign Language.
- I feel my family don't understand and always ask about her next operation. That's all they see; they don't ask about her.
- The only one who listens is my mum; other family members are not even deaf aware. This makes things very difficult, as they don't understand the difficulties.
- The family compare her to other family members and don't understand how hurtful that is.
- When talking about how her needs make me feel, I'm constantly met with, 'At least it's not life threatening,' which makes me feel

guilty about my feelings, and that I'm making a mountain out of a molehill.

- I've chosen to give up my professional career so that I can fully support her and be there to go to all appointments, which is hard on us financially.
- It's draining looking after all the equipment; making sure she can hear and can be understood; always repeating myself; always projecting my voice; always having the TV loud; looking out for cars, bikes etc.
- I worry about the impact on learning/life; I'm always worrying.
- There are added expenses: bottles, formula, cleaning equipment, appointments, fuel, parking, time off work.
- I've had to add her radio aid to the house insurance in order to use it outside of school. This has increased our monthly payments, but we don't own the equipment.
- I had to fight for the radio aid – it feels like everything is a fight.
- I'm always chasing appointments and follow-ups.
- Although the professionals know the medical side, it feels like they forget that she is my whole world and not just another patient. I don't do this as a job, day in and day out; but I do know my child better than anyone and that counts for something.
- It's very hard when the medical team contradict themselves.
- The worst time of my life is when she goes down for her operations – time stands still. It's horrible to see her in so much pain and I feel very helpless.
- I'd swap places with her in a heartbeat.

Q: How do other people react/communicate with your child? Is this different from how people typically interact with a child?

- Nursery were really understanding and helpful. But school don't see or understand her needs, and have hindered her help and support.
- School don't take it seriously because she is so well behaved. I'm told at pick-up that her radio aid wasn't working all afternoon, but they were too busy to change the battery – they said she could hear. If that's the case, why does she have hearing aids and a radio

> aid? They are not equipped to say that she can hear – just because she manages, why should she? Hers is a hidden disability.
> - Even when you tell adults about her hearing loss, they don't slow down their speech or take the time to face her so that she can lip read; this is the case with family too.
> - Her peers forget and don't understand.
> - Most settings are not deaf aware and don't understand the impact on the deaf.
> - Words can be misheard; she has to work so much harder than a hearing person and this takes more energy.
> - When you tell people she is deaf, most people just talk louder!
> - There is an assumption that because she wears hearing aids and has the radio aid, she can hear like a hearing person. But this equipment just amplifies all sounds, which is very draining.

It is so powerful to hear about the experiences of families and children impacted by communication difficulties and there is real value in reflecting on these case studies. Read this mum's words and then read them again. Families frequently use words such as 'fight', 'blame', and 'assumption'. We must reflect on our roles as educators, health professionals and teachers; and we must be aware of the language that we use in our conversations with parents. Are we listening without judgement? Are we communicating effectively and working with parents/carers, always remembering that they are the expert on their own child? When supporting a child with complex communication needs, we must remain vigilant to ensure that we don't disempower families and the child themselves.

It is also important to consider that some children may have difficulties expressing themselves, but have good comprehension skills. We discussed the importance of decision making and autonomy earlier in this chapter. This point is brilliantly illustrated by Communication Disabilities Access Canada, which recorded the impact of communication barriers by interviewing individuals with communication difficulties:

People think that because I can't speak, I can't make my own decisions.

This loss of autonomy was highlighted by adults with communication difficulties; but children with communication difficulties will experience the same issues, so please remember: dignity and respect are crucial.

When children don't respond to our attempts to initiate an interaction or don't communicate spontaneously, it can be a natural response to ask questions or even to step in quickly to help them communicate so that we can get the interaction going. However, the reality is that this in fact can result in the child communicating less, as they feel under pressure. Children are very sensitive to pressure and are aware when we are playing with them to fulfil our own agenda (eg, to assess them; to hear them talk) and when we are genuinely interested in connecting with them and playing together.

Please take the time to read this very powerful account of being a mum to a child with selective mutism:

The first time I heard the term 'selective mutism', my son was two years old. Only a few weeks previously, his key person at playgroup had asked me if he could talk. I was a little baffled by this, as my son had hit all the typical developmental milestones, including his speech development; so why, a few months into starting playgroup, was I being asked if he could talk? It was at this stage that playgroup explained that my son had not spoken one word since he joined the setting; and a few conversations later, it was suggested that we explore selective mutism.

Over the following year, we referred my son to the speech and language therapy service and the educational psychology service, and quite quickly he received a diagnosis of selective mutism. During those 12 months, my son's selective mutism also became progressively worse. He became mute with everyone outside of our immediate family of five, unable to speak to even close family members, such as his auntie and grandparents. Most concerningly for me at this stage, as well as being unable to speak in the majority of social situations, he also became extremely anxious.

Through his early years, acknowledgement and acceptance of my son's condition, for both ourselves and our wider family, became the most important element for him to make progress. To allow my son to thrive, it was important that we accepted him for who he was. We quickly learned that selective mutism is not widely understood. People would comment to us frequently, 'He's just very shy,' or, 'I'm sure he'll grow out of it.' Many people also mistakenly believed that my son was choosing not to speak – that he was being stubborn or rude – not understanding that the selective mutism actually made it impossible for him to speak. Most people had great intentions, but it is a complex condition and as a result it could be really difficult to find people to talk to who could truly relate and understand, resulting in it feeling very lonely at times as a parent. I am forever grateful for my friends, and my son's peers, who accepted him for exactly who he was, whether he was able to speak in front of them or not. These were the same people who got to celebrate his later successes with us when their endless patience paid off.

During my son's preschool and primary school years, he would often appear frozen and unresponsive, compared to the happy, often noisy little boy he was at home. I worried constantly during these years. I worried when I waved him goodbye in the morning, knowing I was potentially leaving him to experience hours of anxiety and silence. I worried about how he would make friends if he was unable to connect with his peers through speech. I worried about how he would ask to go to the toilet, or tell someone he was lost or feeling unwell, if he was unable to speak to his educators. I also had many sleepless nights worrying that people would blame me for my son's selective mutism. Would others think I was a bad parent? (At times I even wondered this myself.) Would people think my son must have had a traumatic experience; think he was being intentionally defiant, or was simply being rude?

As someone whose 'day job' is in education, I felt lucky to have an initial amount of knowledge to be able to access the right support for my son; but I also felt an immense sense of pressure that I should know how to help him win this battle with silence. I felt an overwhelming sense of responsibility to advocate for his needs; to be his voice when he was unable to use his. There was also a constant 'ticking timer' type feeling, as it is well documented that the longer the behavioural patterns of selective mutism develop over time, the more ingrained they become; and in turn they become harder to treat.

I've always believed that with knowledge comes power, so I set out to learn everything I could possibly learn about selective mutism to ensure that my son did not have to continue to struggle in silence. One of the biggest turning points for us was when I began to understand that the fundamental nature of selective mutism is anxiety. When my son's body became swamped with fear and anxiety, his vocal cords would freeze (In later years he would actually describe to us that it felt like someone was squeezing his neck so the words couldn't come out). Speech therefore could not be possible until his anxiety was reduced, so we began a new holistic approach to his 'treatment': we identified his areas of passion and success, and we built on those. For my son, this was, and continues to be, football. Football is more than a hobby for my son: it's his safe space, where he can feel completely comfortable and be entirely himself. Finding my son's passion allowed an outlet into building his self-confidence and reducing his anxiety, and football later became a secure environment in which he would eventually begin to talk to his coach and teammates. We haven't always got it right along the way; experience can be the best and most challenging teacher. However, finding a hobby that 'relaxed' my son certainly has always felt like a breakthrough moment in his journey to free his voice.

There have been lots of tears shed over the years – always mine, never my son's. Something that has always made me feel emotional as a parent of a child with communication difficulties is how my son cannot outwardly express his emotions. I haven't seen my son cry since he was a baby. Due to the anxiety element of selective mutism, he doesn't display any emotions that may draw attention to himself, such as crying or even laughing. I, on the other hand, have sobbed at every significant hurdle we have faced; as well as every achievement throughout his journey, as the enormity of each milestone hit me at how incredibly brave he had needed to be to achieve even the smallest of steps.

Transitions have always been key points in my son's journey, although often the most nerve-wracking times for us all have been the key to significant progress. We always knew from research that a new school could be the key to unlocking my son's voice. The lack of 'expectation of silence' in a new setting can make it easier for a child to speak, so times of transition have always felt like high-pressure situations. I can honestly say that sitting in my son's senior school appeal meeting was the most anxious I have ever felt in my life. I knew deep down that winning the appeal, and my son gaining a place at the school he had chosen as his first preference, could be a 'make or break' situation for him being able to use his voice in his teenage years and beyond. As I sat there overwhelmed by anxiety, the thought that gave me the confidence to give my absolute all to appealing his case was the knowledge that how I felt in that moment is how my son felt every single day of his young life; yet he always had the courage to face every day and be as brave as he could possibly be. We won the appeal, and my son 'found his voice' on the very first day of senior school!

It's a scary thing to say my son has 'overcome his selective mutism', as it has a sense of tempting fate. I don't believe that I will ever not be concerned that something may cause the mutism to return, but since joining senior school my son is now able to speak in nearly all social situations. I asked my son if he would like to contribute to his story with his own words but he was absolutely adamant he didn't want to – even all these years later, he isn't ready to talk about his journey with selective mutism. My son has rarely talked about how it feels to have selective mutism; often when asked, he becomes significantly distressed. Sometimes after a visit from a supporting professional, he wouldn't talk to me for days, as he would blame me for their involvement. Sometimes we don't always get the balance right; but we quickly learned that our home had to be, and continues to be, his safe place, where he can truly be himself.

Overcoming my son's selective mutism as a family was a journey – a rollercoaster of ups and downs, pain and perseverance. As parents, it has been emotional and frustrating; however, it has also been a rewarding path of gaining understanding and it has certainly made us more considerate of others' hidden challenges. It's a journey I think we will always be on in some way, but my son continues to be the most courageous person I know. It has taken immense bravery, over many years, to become the 16-year-old boy he is today. The challenges he has faced in his earlier years have shaped him into the most considerate, caring, kind-natured young man, with an incredible sense of humour. He is now predicted to pass all his GCSEs and is about to embark on the next step of his journey into post-16 education. He has developed close friendships at every stage of his life, despite being unable to use speech consistently until senior school age. Witnessing the incredible progress he has made over recent years, now he has found his voice, has opened my eyes to what amazing potential was trapped under his inability to effectively communicate for so many years. So many people could make a significant difference to the wellbeing, learning and futures of those with communication difficulties through simply taking the time to understand and educate themselves, while demonstrating a little kindness and patience. I am incredibly proud of my son and will continue to be his advocate, supporting him in unlocking his full potential every day; only now he can join me and use the power of his own voice too.

This brave and honest account is very powerful and gives us insight into the complex nature of selective mutism. It also illustrates the impact of a communication difficulty on an individual and also their wider family.

It is so important that we hear these real-life accounts and take time to reflect and understand the impact of SLCN, as this will help us to shape our interactions and support in a way that is meaningful for each individual.

Mine Conkbayir (2023) explains clearly:

Effective communication also needs to be woven throughout all our interactions with children, not only for modelling purposes but to make them feel respected, listened to and safe. Through this reciprocal exchange, children can gradually build trust, which is vital in enabling children to relax and understand what is being said and to encourage them to reach out and express their thoughts and feelings.

This ... this is what children need from us!

For many children, communication develops without the need for any targeted interventions; but we also know that there are approximately 1.7 million children struggling with talking and understanding words in the UK (Speech and Language UK).

'Neurodiversity' is a term which has become widely used since it was coined by Judy Singer in the mid-1990s. The term acknowledges that every brain is different; and from this concept came the terms 'neurotypical' and 'neurodivergent'. 'Neurodivergent' refers to how people experience and interact with the world around them in many different ways, and that this variation is not viewed as 'wrong' or 'deficient.' The most common types of neurodivergence include:

* Autism.
* Attention deficit hyperactivity disorder.
* Dyslexia.

- Developmental coordination disorder/dyspraxia.
- DLD.

Diagnosis is often a long and detailed process, and can help us to understand why a child may need adaptations to the environment in order for them to realise their potential and access learning; but we must always remember to *see the child and not their diagnosis*. Our role is to know all the children in our settings and to understand what their superpowers are and what they may be finding difficult.

We are hopeful that attitudes in society are changing and evolving as we understand more about how the brain works, and how differences make us neither more important or less significant than others. The language used around neurodivergence is ever changing, with some people even challenging the use of the term 'neurodivergence' itself; so it is really important to keep researching and do our best to use language which is respectful and informed. For some individuals, a 'diagnosis' can result in a sense of identity and belonging. Our advice would be to ask the individual how they refer to themselves and how they would like us to refer to them in any communications we make.

Communication and Interaction Toolkit

Our Communication and Interaction Toolkit consists of strategies and techniques which can be used to communicate with all children, but which will really benefit those children with the challenge of SLCN:

- **Positioning:** Position yourself at the same level as the child. This shows them that you are there with them and ready to connect. When you are at the same level as the child, you can see each other's faces more easily, which helps you both to observe facial expressions and other non-verbal communication. Please be aware that eye contact is not comfortable for all individuals, so do not put any pressure on the child to establish this. Making it easier for the child to see your face also provides opportunity for the child to see how your mouth is moving when you speak, offering good role modelling of speech sounds.

- **Time, space, pace:** Give the child time to process language. Children who struggle to understand language will need more time to work out what you have said to them. Break information down into smaller 'chunks' to make it easier to understand and stress key words.

  Wait to be invited into the child's play and wait to give the child time to initiate an interaction. Some children will be able to do this using words but others won't have words, so look for subtle communication cues – eye pointing, gestures and body language.

  Give the child space to be themselves. Observe their patterns of play, as this will give you more information about what matters to the child and will help you to understand how to connect with them in a way that is meaningful to them.

  Use the space to understand how the child is communicating. This may be verbally, but it also may be through gesture, vocalisation and other behaviours. We need to know how the child is communicating so that we can interact and communicate in a way that will be understood by the child. Be aware of your own communication style, and know that you may need to adapt your communication and interaction skills in order to connect with the child.

  Pace your interactions. Be aware of the language load we are expecting the child to process, and be aware of when to join play and when to step back and allow the child's play to flow and develop independently.
- **Follow the child's lead:** When we let the child lead the play, we show them that we value their ideas. Children will be more motivated to communicate about things that interest them; and when we follow their lead, we can give them the opportunity to communicate their thoughts and ideas through play.

  Be aware that children do not all play in the same way. Be aware of when you change the child's play. Often we have good intentions to 'teach' and show the child how they could play, but we need to be careful not to 'take over.' We can look at the play and offer other resources which may extend the child's ideas, but we must resist the urge to lead, as this will stifle the child's play and creativity.
- **Comment:** Make natural comments which match what is happening for the child. You can comment on their play or on sounds/sights in the environment. When we comment on what is happening, we are teaching new vocabulary and introducing new ideas and concepts.

Just be mindful not to saturate with words. Natural comments are really useful, but a constant narrative may be a bit frustrating for the child and key vocabulary may be lost in the strings of words.

Comments are more useful than asking lots of questions. We don't need to ask questions when we already know the answer. 'What colour is this?' This type of question serves no purpose other than to 'test' the child and we certainly don't need to be doing that!

MINDFUL MOMENT...

Spend some time observing your colleagues. If you work alone, see if you can link up with other educators for some peer observation.

Observe each other for ten to 15 minutes, interacting and playing with children. Keep a tally of how many questions the adult asks during this short play session. You may be surprised by how many questions you are asking. Can you think of examples where questions asked during play could be turned into a comment?

- **Extend:** You can use your communication skills to extend what a child is saying/expressing. If a child is using sounds to communicate, you can build on this. For example, if a child playing with a car says, 'Brrrrmmm,' you can build on this by responding with, 'Car goes brrrrmmm.'

  If a child is using single words to communicate, you can extend this by repeating back what they say and adding another word. For example, if a child pops a bubble and says 'Pop,' you can extend by saying, 'Bubble pop.'

  We are not expecting the child to copy us, but we are showing the child how to build their language skills naturally, through play.
- **Find the connection:** To us, this is the most important strategy to understand. Some children are skilled at developing relationships, while others may appear to 'shut the world out'. Our role is to 'connect'. We find connections by knowing the child, observing how they play and explore their environment, and knowing when we can gently approach and enter the child's world. What this looks like will vary depending

on the child; we must remember that every child is unique and this is especially true when a diagnosis has been given.

We are always cautious about giving 'advice on how to communicate and interact with a specific group of children – for example, how to communicate with autistic children. The reason is simple and has already been stated: **every child is unique**, even when they share a diagnosis, and there are no set 'rules' on how we should communicate and interact with them. What is essential is that we work to find a connection.

Once we create moments of connection, we can really start to understand who the child is and what matters to them. This could be a specific interest, such as dinosaurs; it could be exploring the outside by running, climbing and jumping; or it could be exploring different textures using their mouth and hands. What is important is that we are not trying to change children from who they truly are – we are just seeking to understand them more, so that we can communicate and interact with them in a meaningful way.

The 'communication connection' is when the child realises that their communication has meaning and power. This then gives them the motivation to use these skills and develop further. This matters because children need a reason to communicate, a desire to do so and a responsive person to interact with. Seek advice from a speech and language therapist about how to support the child in making the 'communication connection.'

Summary

Learning to talk is a complicated process. Adults can support this process by being active listeners, following the child's interests and observing the child's communication attempts. Adults can also inhibit the development of this process if they are not aware of the importance of quality interactions.

Being able to communicate our needs and wants, and to be listened to, is a basic human right. For those who struggle to communicate, it is our duty to adapt our environment and reflect on our interactions to enable them to have a voice, however they are communicating.

Further reading and research ideas

ADHD UK
www.adhduk.co.uk

National Autistic Society
www.autism.org.uk

BBC, *Tiny Happy People*
www.bbc.co.uk/tiny-happy-people

British Dyslexia Association
www.bdadyslexia.org.uk

British Stammering Association
www.stamma.org

Cleft Lip and Palate Association
www.clapa.com

Elklan Training
www.elklan.co.uk

Early Years TV
www.earlyyears.tv

The Hanen Centre
www.hanen.org

Selective Mutism Information & Research Association
www.selectivemutism.org.uk

Speech and Language UK
www.speechandlanguage.org.uk

Thriving Language Podcasts
www.thrivinglanguage.co.uk

Creating environments in which all children are understood

How does the environment impact on communication and wellbeing?

Throughout this book, we have explored the role of the educator as a crucial part of the environment. We must always see ourselves as creating the environment, wherever we work. What does it feel like to be a child or a colleague in your setting?

When we think of environments, we are thinking deeply about the atmosphere that we and others create. You can feel it: it's tangible. You can notice minuscule changes with just a glance, which can set a new and different feeling, changing the context for each person within it. This is where we see that communication is key to wellbeing and to ensuring that everyone can thrive.

We must consider how our communications are perceived and understood. We must be honest, true and responsive when we see harmful communications towards our colleagues and the children we work with. This does not mean we react; it means we respond and speak to managers and colleagues, using the correct procedures and daily evaluations. The question we must always ask ourselves is: what did that feel like for the child? What valuable and research-based understanding was developed with the child; and what was happening to their emotional brain development? Were the child's feelings and brain connections considered in the response from the adult?

DOI: 10.4324/9781003335429-5

Remember, the environment creates an impression and experience for us all. This may not be visible, but we know what it feels like to be encompassed in a genuine atmosphere of love and care. Children are experts from birth at understanding atmospheres and connections (Zeedyk 2020; Benoit 2004; Solihull Approach 2002). This is what helps to keep them safe and well, and is how their brain connections develop. As educators and adults in a prime position of responsibility for fostering children's emotional wellbeing and advancing their brain development, we must champion the child's rights and always advocate for the child to be themselves in their environment. The child's communication style must be met and understood, and then built upon by educators. Educators must be tuned in, and notice and connect with the child's little glances and indications. From here, we can start to form relationships that underpin the foundations for lifelong communication and emotional wellbeing to thrive.

United Nations Convention on the Rights of the Child

Article 12 of the United Nations Convention on the Rights of the Child enshrines the rights of children to be listened to and taken seriously:

> *Every child has the right to express their views, feelings and wishes in all matters affecting them, and to have their views considered and taken seriously. This right applies at all times, for example during immigration proceedings, housing decisions or the child's day-to-day home life.*

Article 13 enshrines the child's right to freedom of expression:

> *Every child must be free to express their thoughts and opinions and to access all kinds of information, as long as it is within the law.*

It is worth delving into these provisions further and exploring the rights of children to understand what these look like in your environment – for the children, for you and for your colleagues. This is a wonderful place from which to reflect, to see how children's rights inform your everyday practice. Use resources that are interactive, touchable, intriguing and visible, so that children know and understand their rights as a child from an early age. Sharing these with all adults who care for, live with or work with children helps to advocate for, and bring understanding to, the voice of the child.

MINDFUL MOMENT...

Throughout our daily lives, we will experience new and varied environments: familiar, comforting, unreceptive or even hostile. Have a think about your experiences and how you feel in the following everyday spaces:

- What does it feel like to go to the doctor's?
- What does it feel like to go to the dentist's?
- What does it smell like in the supermarket?
- What does the dynamic feel like at your favourite restaurant?
- When you are in an unfamiliar environment, what helps you to relax and thrive?
- Why do you like going to certain places and not others?
- How do environments in everyday life make you feel?
- Have you ever been a bit confused at the train station, the airport or the garage, and someone has helped you? How did this make you feel? We hope it was a great response that made you feel safe – that you felt you mattered and were worth being listened to.
- We can all think of times where we have not felt that our communications were heard; how did you feel about this and what did you do?

The Reggio Emilia approach, developed under the guidance of Loris Malaguzzi, posits that the environment is the third 'teacher' in the fundamental triangle of learning, together with the family and educators. From this, we can see the profound importance that the role of the environment plays in creating the optimum learning space for all children. To create environments in which communication and wellbeing can thrive, we should first explore the principal factors in creating conditions in which children can blossom, and where this is the uppermost priority of all their educators.

How to create 'safe spaces' where children can thrive

The very simple answer to this is to be kind, loving, consistent and connected.

A more rounded answer is to meet children's needs when they need you; to communicate on their level with interest and intrigue; to extend their play through their ideas; to continue researching the vital role of the educator; and to offer love and comfort. All of this will enable the child to be themselves and have self-worth. This doesn't mean that the child will never question or become upset or angry; it means that their emotional needs are listened to. Your skill as an educator who understands that children learn when they feel safe will be to teach the child that their emotions are an important part of their own life and the lives of others. We do not eradicate every problem that occurs; we just help to smooth the bumps on the road that the child is travelling. By doing this, we help them to develop the skills and emotional intelligence that they will need now, as teens and as adults to cope with their life experiences.

CASE STUDY

Let's look at this connection and communication journey between an educator and a child. The educator in this case study is new to a setting and discusses her thoughts, observations and reflections:

When starting at a new setting, I was aware of one child who appeared to be wary of adults and peers. The child was noticeably quiet and would look at adults very cautiously. I felt it was because perhaps she didn't trust anyone and I believed she didn't feel safe. I wanted to form a relationship with her, and for her to feel safe with me and start to trust others. When I first tried to play with her, she would keep at a distance and often would not use words to communicate. She would point to what she wanted. One day I was playing with her at the water tray with some other children when she snatched a cup from another child, who began to cry. We had a chat about sharing our cups and that we can find more cups; but she was quite cross with me. I reassured her that everything was okay, and in that moment I just asked if she wanted a cuddle. She did want a cuddle and I was so pleased that she wanted some comfort from me. Over the next two weeks, she became chattier with me and often came for cuddles. We then had a school holiday and she was away for three weeks. On the day she came back, she came running in with a beaming smile, shouting, 'Hello!' and jumped on me for a cuddle! Yes! I finally felt we had a relationship and she was pleased to see me. I told her how happy I was to see her, and our friendship has continued to grow since then. She appears much happier and is smiley in school and is so kind to her friends. I found the cuddles have really formed better communication and comfort, and she feels safer with me. Now she can start to play and learn.

MINDFUL MOMENT...

What are your thoughts?

- What made the biggest difference to the child?
- How was the child's communication supported?
- What do you think were the key points in the child's journey?
- Why does the child feel safer?
- Do you think the child now trusts that her communications will be heard and understood?
- What did the environment feel like for the child at the start of her journey and what might it feels like now?

Creating communication-rich environments

Physical spaces for children should feel relaxing, welcoming, comforting and intriguing. It is crucial that children feel safe, loved and understood in their everyday spaces. Communications should be accepted as they are seen and heard, then built upon through the physical and emotional connections you create.

Does your space have sofas on which communications and connections can be grown together, or blankets in which you can snuggle up and read together? Connective communication grows and develops when a child feels included, and that the space is just as much theirs as the adults'. A good way of thinking about this is: are you all in this together? Who has ownership of the space? Who makes the decisions on what the next roleplay will be? Who chooses what to have at snack time? You get the idea: when you feel you have a choice in decisions about your own life, you feel included and understood.

Children who are included in decision making can become independent learners who know that their own ideas and those of others matter. They develop the ability to communicate their thoughts, knowing that they will be listened to. This doesn't mean everything will always go the way we might want it to; it does mean that ideas are valued and discussed. We can recognise disappointment when ideas do not come to fruition and can use this as a talking and learning point: 'I know it's disappointing. I wanted the big tent out too – I can see you are cross about that.' These are genuine conversations, which recognise how the child might be feeling in the time and at the pace the child needs. Remember that we are educators, and our role is to develop emotional intelligence and empathy with our children. There is no rush here: our children deserve the best lessons in life and these take time.

You are building the foundations of the child's brain with them right now (Zeedyk 2020), and this is definitely worth a huge chunk of your time. As educators and adults, we have a responsibility to know why and how we practise, and what effect this has on the child's developing brain.

In creating environments with children's wellbeing at heart, we must consider the importance of the connections we create and the vast research around neuroscience in the early years. This often highlights the fundamental role of the educator. We can observe this in Dr Mine Conkbayir's interview with Dr Stuart Shanker in *The Neuroscience of the Developing Child*, which emphasises *that children learn best when they and their educators feel emotionally and physically safe, and the stresses they are exposed to are positive and enriching.*

MINDFUL MOMENT...

What helps you and the children in your environment to feel emotionally and physically safe?

When we practise and educate with this in mind, we can create open, natural and trusting communications and connections.

How do you feel about the outside and inside environments?

It is vital to understand our role, our thoughts and our power as an educator in the environment. For example, think about decision making: who decides what weather you can go outside in? How do the educators and children feel about outside? Some people love to go out, while others don't. Most of us adults have a choice and we exercise this. We know the many benefits of being outside – there is oodles of research on this; however, some children still only spend about an hour a day outside.

Long periods of time are spent inside; but there is little research suggesting that this is a good place for children to be for protracted lengths of time. So how can educators embrace the outdoors, and the wellbeing and communication opportunities it presents for children? Again, by being honest and reflective. We are educators who understand that children need to spend more time outdoors to engage deeply; so we will need to wrap up with layers and take turns being outdoors.

Now, as we just observed, some people love being outside and may embrace the chance to be out more; they may also be much happier – and teach to the best of their ability – in an outdoor environment. It makes sense to enable those people to be outdoors; just remember to check in with them every so often, to ensure that this is still the case. If you are an educator who likes being inside, then you can embrace that environment; but try to have positive energy about all areas, as the children will look to you for guidance. All educators need to think about their phrasing around the weather:

'Is it a dull day?' 'Is it too cold to go outside?' 'Is it okay to wish winter days away?' 'Is it horrible wet weather?' How we speak to children and what we say within earshot build the foundations of what they think about the world. This is a big responsibility, we know, and one that we must take very seriously. We are educators; we are professionals; and we must appreciate that children learn from what we say.

When we really observe where children play and where they are most engaged, we can then identify the unused spaces in the setting and reflect on why these areas are not so popular (Poulter Jewson and Skinner 2022).

What are the benefits of different environments?

A simple answer is that the best environment is wherever the children are allowed to have time to play and are supported by educators who treasure them. A more in-depth suggestion is that we can look around the world to see what happens in other environments around the world.

We love the Danish idea and ethos of *hygge* ('hoo-gah'). *Hygge* is described by Meik Wiking (2016), the chief executive of the Happiness Research Institution in Copenhagen, as:

Creating an atmosphere where you can let your guard down.

What does it feel like to create and be in an environment where you can all just be yourselves and go with the flow? It may also be useful to consider how we can apply this in our professional and educational environment (Csikszentmihalyi 2008). We should reflect on the fact that Denmark has a Happiness Research Institution: how amazing is it that the Danish people are held in mind and their happiness is seen as fundamental to their society? In recent studies (WHR 2022; HDI 2022), Denmark was ranked the second-happiest country in the world. You could take a more in-depth look to discover why this is and explore what enables environments of happiness, connections and security.

Educators are building these environments daily for children, so more information is always helpful in developing our ideas and the research behind our practice. We have also written about the Reggio Emilia district of Italy and its influence on practice with the child at heart. These are tried-and-tested ways to enable children to grow. Educators do not stagnate in their ideas; they keep moving forward and always keep the bigger picture in mind.

Children are the influencers and creators of our society, now and in the future. We, the adults and educators, are their guardians at this present time: we have the power to evoke change; to be kind; to listen and create connections every single day.

Early years environments are most definitely places of laughter – don't let anyone persuade you otherwise! By creating fun and enjoyment together, the child will love to play and will feel safe, and their wellbeing and development will flow. This will help to build connections and relationships, promoting authentic interactions within your environments.

Let's take a look at the research on why spending time outside is much more than just a breath of fresh air. Playing outside is good for children's mental and physical health; you can discover more about this in an article entitled 'Do you have a gut feeling that being outdoors is healthy?' (Goldberg 2022). Naturalistic research studies have examined the impact of the outdoor environment on children's stress levels, attention spans, learning and behaviour, including speech and language. One study by Gemma Goldberg sought to understand what happens for young children by monitoring heart and brain activity (Goldberg, Skinner and Poulter Jewson 2022 – podcast).

There is one school of thought in early years education that children should be encouraged to sit still and learn, so that they will be able to do this in the classroom. However, studies have shown that the exact opposite is in fact required: children who play outside for longer periods of time are less likely to be inattentive or hyperactive (Ulset 2017; cited by Goldberg 2022). The research on 'school readiness' indicates that it is not necessary to make children sit down or sit still to prepare them for school. Children are physical, social people who need to experience learning with their whole sense of self, and to communicate their ideas through their body language and their interactions in the way they choose, and in an environment that supports this.

There are several ways in which we can access the outdoors to create richer communication and wellbeing spaces. It's true, you do need to work with the environment you have; but you can always bring the outside in. By this, we mean exploring natural materials, which affords great experiences and natural language prompts. When we explore objects that are interesting and new, we learn different concepts and add to our knowledge bank. As educators, we are commenting naturally on what the children are experiencing – just as you would if you found things while beachcombing on a beach. For example, you could assemble a tray of soil, fir branches, pinecones, feathers, conkers and so on, which children can explore throughout their play inside. In this way, you can bring a little of their outside world inside to discover. Sand, water and clay are all materials that children can have to hand and use in every session to continue to explore and develop their thoughts and ideas. This is how communication can thrive holistically, enabling new discussions and ideas to unfold together.

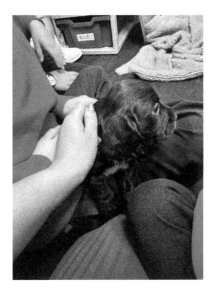

Real life is great for creating new depths of understanding: nothing compares to real-life experiences when it comes to building connections and communications.

MINDFUL MOMENT...

Real-life resources

Think about what different textures, such as rubber, wooden, plastic or natural brick:

- What are the differences and similarities you experience?
- What different weights do you feel?
- How can you build and create in different ways?
- If you had never felt or touched a real house brick, would you really understand what it is?
- How can you enhance communication by using real objects?

Let's consider how to extend ideas when a child is interested in building. Have you tried using sand and real bricks? (You could easily chop these in half to make them more manageable.) The children can mix sand and water and explore laying the 'cement' using trowels. In doing so, they can learn that buildings need strength and solid foundations to stand. As educators, our role is not to tell them the consistency of the mixture: they should discover this through play, comments, trial and error, in an environment that trusts them, and that trusts play.

Once the children have experienced play for some time, we can come up with a mix together with them. If we began the provocation by giving instructions on how to create a sand and water mix – for example, one cup of water to three cups of sand – and then continued to show them how to make the mix, we would be doing all the thinking for the children. When we do all the thinking, we miss great opportunities for the children to make enquiries, ask questions and test out their ideas in practice through natural experimentation.

Supporting provocation and adding in numbers and comments at the right time in play are skills we can master by observing and extending, without adulterating play. Remember, children have their own ideas and will communicate these when they know that their thoughts and words are valued and understood. By all means, do play alongside them and create experiments together; but follow the child's lead and wait to be invited in. Deep levels of engagement

Time   Play   Explore   Connect   Provocation

Figure 4.1 Creating environments where children can thrive, connect and communicate
Source: Thriving Language 2023

in play create connections in children's brains. This will happen when you give them time to work things out through play, with attuned adults at hand to add provocation and support their ideas at the right time.

Let's now discuss free-flow accessibility. What do we mean by the term 'free flow'? This is where we provide equal access to outside and inside throughout the whole day, giving children a real choice in deciding where to play. Spending big chunks of time outside will enable them to become deeply engaged. The 'flow' of a child's play is when they are completely engaged. When this flow is uninterrupted by adults in the setting, they enter a deeper state of learning and this leads to increased and stronger connections in the brain (Bruce 1991). Children require outdoors environments where they can build on their own interactions and those of others, and develop their ideas and imaginations through their 'personal spaces', which link to the child's identity (Garric, 2009).

MINDFUL MOMENT...

Csikszentmihalyi describes 'flow' as:

a state in which people are so involved in an activity that nothing else seems to matter; the experience is so enjoyable that people will continue to do it even at great cost, for the sheer sake of doing it (1990).

- Do you ever experience a flow state of mind?
- Can you see why children really don't want to stop what they are doing?
- What would it feel like to keep being interrupted when you were in full flow?

You can discover more about this theory and see how it relates to your practice and children's communicational play and behaviours.

Educators and adults in a child's world must always advocate for the importance of play and understand that play is learning.

Although learning takes place throughout life, in early childhood, learning is taking place at a speed that will never be equalled.

Unicef 2018

AN EDUCATOR'S EXPERIENCE...

Let's look at how environments for communication and connections can be created. This educator is an experienced early years lead and a qualified forest school and early years teacher. She is in tune with the children, families and colleagues with whom she communicates and interacts:

When planning for communication within the forest school environment, I consider how the space can be used by the children. Looking at it from their perspective and with a sense of fun and adventure, I look for the spaces with many possibilities.

Where children choose to play can only be known through observation. I ensure that there are social spaces available in which children can gather, such as the mud kitchen, where they can watch each other as they make their latest mud cake; accessible, hidden places like cosy dens where they can squeeze in together; and areas with resources which can be moved (eg, a trail of toy animals) or used for construction, giving them the opportunity to bring others into their play.

Having the ability to change the way a space looks fosters a sense of ownership and builds knowledge of self and others, and the space they're in. This ability to explore the possibilities, and the presence of wildlife to be observed and cared for, make these enriching social experiences.

Furthermore, these types of hands-on experiences lead to a greater connection with nature.

The most important aspect of the provision is giving the children the time and space to explore these areas in their own time and in their own way. At forest school, building trust in relationships is key and supporting children in building connections helps develop trust.

MINDFUL MOMENT...

What are your thoughts?

- Are the children's ideas trusted?
- How is the child's communication supported?
- What do you think it would feel like to work and play in this space?
- Would the child feel safe and listened to?
- What does the physical environment feel like for the child?
- What does the emotional environment feel like for the child?
- Is deep engagement in play encouraged and respected?
- How are child-to-child connections supported?
- Can you observe how planning and reflection are interwoven with the child at the centre?

Think about your physical space: what does it feel like when you walk in? Is it intriguing? Does it provoke natural comments and questions? A little note on the lighting: try turning the big lights off – especially strip lighting – and putting fairy lights on instead (do ensure these have been safety tested). The difference that subtle lighting makes to everyone's mood is great for promoting wellbeing and relaxation. It might seem like a cliché, but it really is valuable to take time to study your environment, see what it looks like from a child's perspective and spend five minutes a day decluttering.

Children learn from their environments: how they look and feel has a major impact on the child's taught and learned experiences. Bring in as much fresh air and natural light as possible. Children love helping to clean windows and this can make a dramatic difference to the light that floods in; clear windows without anything on them is a great place to start. Let the children be creative with natural products – encourage them to explore, to create, to make mixtures. We most definitely aren't saying don't be messy; but taking care of their environment from a young age will help the children in caring for and sustaining not only their personal space, but also their wider community and the planet.

Try to leave pictures and collages out for them to build on daily. Using an actual canvas, rather than just lots of paper, means you will then have a body of work developed over weeks and months to display. We don't know what the end product will look like and that's just how it should be: the children's ideas should change and evolve as they develop their thoughts. Further research that could inspire you include the Montessori, Froebel and Reggio Emilia approaches.

Patterns of play and communication in the environment

Notice what children are doing and investigating, so that an appropriate curriculum which matches children's lines of enquiries and capabilities is offered.

Brock 2022

One of the most important things we should seek to understand and unpick is how the child is exploring their environment.

* What are their actions telling us?
* What is their nonverbal communication showing us?
* What is their verbal communication expressing to us?
* What do they do to keep themselves busy?
* What is intriguing and engaging them so much that you know to disturb them would change their play?

When we see a child's eyes light up, and we notice that they are intrigued by something they are doing or observing in their environment, this is when we know they are interested. This teaches us all about themselves and how they learn: their body language will tell us all we need to know. As educators, we all understand that observing children is vital – it is one of the greatest ways to learn what they are thinking and what makes sense to them in their world. It is like having a little key which unlocks the patterns of play that the child has been showing us: we have opened our eyes and noticed their schematic play and ideas. How great does it feel when you know that someone is interested in your ideas?

What does a child's pattern of play tell us about how they learn and express themselves?

Children use their patterns of play, their schema and schemes, in every element of their curriculum. So, for example, if a child likes to cover themselves up and snuggle up in dens, you may find that they like to paint their fingernails or paint all the way up their arms. They may like hide-and-seek games and *The Mole in the Hole* storybook. They may like books that have flaps with all sorts of things hiding underneath them. They may like sitting under a table. The main point here is to offer resources that support and build on their ideas. Noticing is one element; supporting and offering provocation is where your skill comes in. 'I noticed you like to hide – would you like to make a den with these sticks outside?' 'I wondered if you would like to help create a bed for the hedgehogs to hibernate?' What else is the child interested in and how can you support this, so that each child's patterns of play and interests become the most important part of your curriculum?

Think about the intriguing things that children bring to school with them. Does one child always play with the same toy? Do they want to do the same puzzle every time? Are they fascinated by the water tap? Is there one child who loves to throw things, and another who loves to twirl themselves around and around? Do some children just want to run around? Do some children like to pick up little things up and carry them around? Are there some children who are very accurate in their drawings and others who paint all over everything?

Have you recognised any of the children you work with in these examples? If so, that's great: this is where you build communications from and understand what children are trying to tell you. If you haven't started to spot patterns of play in your setting, have a look now that you know a little more and start to support this play in your environment.

All children are individuals, and as educators we have the joy of discovering what interests them and makes them unique.

MINDFUL MOMENT...

How can you create understanding in your environment and build on the child's communications? Let's consider a child who enjoys picking little things up and carrying them around with them.

A quick note here: these are offered provocations only. They are not set in stone; no child must do them, and all children are welcome to have a go and get involved. This will depend on their thoughts about our ideas and whether these tap into their interests. We don't all learn in the same way; however, if we are with someone kind, who is interested in our thoughts and has a flexible agenda, we are more likely to join in and give our views and thoughts. Ta-da! That is another little insight into the child's world: they just shared their ideas and thoughts because we listened and responded.

- Is there time for the child to stop and pick up objects? Could you go on an exploring adventure together? Are there other children who might like to help find things too? These children could have different patterns of play; however, children who like creating with detail or carrying objects around might like to join in.
- How could you build on this together? Might the child like to display their findings? Could they 'curate' their discoveries in a cabinet, shelf, box or drawer, where other people can view and learn about them? Think about developing a language-rich environment: introduce new vocabulary and experiences. For example, consider the statement, 'Archaeologists discover hidden treasures' – where could the child and educator go from here? Where could you visit and what might the child tell you about their discoveries? Could you label their findings, encouraging the child to create labels and information for each item? Could other children 'buy them' in a 'gift shop'? This would involve using numbers and letters for a purpose; you could even use real money. There are endless opportunities to expand and develop these ideas through

to new schemes. The connections being created and developed in the child's brain are crucial both now and for future learning.

- Lynnette Brock and John Siraj-Blatchford (2019) suggest that it is useful to think of a child following a well-trodden footpath in their mind – these schematic 'footpaths' are more accessible for them.
- Immersion in the flow of play creates the opportunities needed for deep engagement, enabling the child to build their brain connections, and to be heard and valued for who they are at the pace they choose to play (Bruce 1991).

Play is the highest expression of human development in childhood for it alone is the free expression of what is in a child's soul.

Froebel, 1782–1852

The role of the adult in the communication environment

 AN EDUCATOR'S EXPERIENCE...

Please take a moment to read the following words from Mandy Johnson, an education professional at the Soul School for Wellbeing:

As an experienced educational practitioner with over 33 years of experience, I wholeheartedly believe that a positive relationship between teacher and student is crucial for their academic and personal growth. A teacher's attitude, actions and approach towards a student can have a profound impact on their perception of themselves, their learning and their overall wellbeing. A teacher who takes the time to connect with the student, understand them as an individual and create a safe and nurturing space for them is invaluable to their development and success.

Research studies have consistently highlighted the positive impact of a strong student-teacher relationship on academic, social and emotional outcomes. When students feel valued and respected, they are more motivated and engaged, leading to better academic performance and a stronger work ethic. Moreover, a positive relationship with a teacher fosters a sense of belonging, self-esteem and positive social interactions, which contributes to their overall wellbeing.

In light of the challenges presented by remote learning, it is more important than ever to prioritize building meaningful connections with students. Educators must adapt their approach to create a dynamic and engaging virtual learning environment that fosters communication, interaction and personalised attention. By providing opportunities for one-on-one interactions, incorporating social and emotional learning and using technology creatively, teachers can maintain a positive relationship with their students and help them to succeed.

In conclusion, a positive relationship between a teacher and a student is the cornerstone of academic and personal growth. Teachers who prioritise building strong relationships with their students create a safe, nurturing and engaging learning environment that fosters student success and wellbeing.

Mandy highlights the importance of the relationship between educator and child, so it is essential that we look after our own wellbeing so that we can be the educators we want to be.

How does an adult's emotional wellbeing impact on the early years environment?

Did you know that children can pick up on emotional tone milliseconds before they process the words we are saying to them? Our emotional tone is what conveys cues of safety or threat to children (Delahooke 2020). Our emotional presence has a dramatic impact on children, and they are experts at reading between the lines and understanding how we really feel.

As educators, we must carry out our role in the certainty that we are helping to teach and develop the children we work with, in a professionally kind and loving manner (Page 2011). Our words, our utterances, the way we look at a child and the tone we use all communicate to them how we actually feel about them, and whether we really understand them and their communications. Dr Sophie Mort (2021) also reminds us that children fare best when their school feels safe, is accepting and nurturing of their personal culture, and meets their physical needs.

We know that working in educational environments where every day is different and where each child and family is unique can be exciting and at times challenging. You need so much energy to physically and emotionally create the desired environment, in which it is not only the children who can thrive, but also you and your colleagues. It is crucial to tune into what you need both as an individual and a part of a team; and to know when you need to stop and are running on empty. Look at the decision of Jacinda Arden, the prime minister of New Zealand, to stand down after five years in office. She knew that she had done enough and that this was the right time for her to prioritise her emotional and physical needs. She demonstrated a deep understanding of the responsibility that comes with the privileged role of prime minister.

Educators are leaders – maybe not of a country, but of thousands of children whose lives they touch. You, as an educator, are in an amazingly privileged position of being one of the key foundations from which children develop. You should not become burned out at their or your expense; knowing when you need to slow down is vital. In our educational and caring profession, we give so much of ourselves daily and often put our own needs on hold. Kate Moxley discusses the key elements of preventing and overcoming burnout, and putting wellbeing heart and centre of your early years pedagogical approach (Moxley 2022). Be mindful of where you are in your journey, and what you need to thrive and flourish. Creating a growth environment for quality interactions and dynamic communications takes time, space and pace (Poulter Jewson and Skinner, 2022). Educators should know themselves well, reflect daily and understand what each child needs to develop.

MINDFUL MOMENT...

It is worth delving into what your early years practice means to you:

- What are your professional boundaries?
- Is there a culture of overworking?
- Is there a culture of professional love and communication?
- Is there a self-perpetuating overload – by this we mean, are you saying 'yes' far too often to extra hours or taking work home?
- Do you feel that your life and work are balanced, and that you have time for yourself?
- Do you have robust supervisions and are these times when you are heard and you can be really honest?
- If you feel tired and overwhelmed, who can you talk too?
- What would you do if you didn't feel well, physically or emotionally, at work – or even before getting to work?

We highly recommend that you read *Creating a Culture of Kindness and Accountability* (Moxley 2022), which explores what this looks like in practice.

Emotional intelligence and wellbeing are paramount for educators. Remember, you are completely worth being cared about and being heard. Your role is one to be valued. The joy that your connections and communications can bring into children's lives will stay with them forever. So ensure that you find joy and emotional wellbeing in your career, and in your communications throughout your daily life too.

Leaders should be kind and strong.

Arden, 2023

Taking the cue from the child

AN EDUCATOR'S EXPERIENCE...

Please take some time to read and reflect on the following words of Schemaplay director Lynnette Brock, who considers how children's observed patterns of behaviours are a form of communication, and think about how you can use this information in your work with children:

To appreciate how we learn through our actions upon the world, it is important to consider the distinction that Piaget made between two words – a 'schema' and a 'scheme':

> *The terms 'scheme' and 'schema' correspond to quite distinct realities, the one operative (a scheme of action/pattern of repeated behaviour) and the other figurative (a 'schema' – an object, word, label or picture)*
>
> *(Piaget, 1969, ix).*

Observing children's operational schemes – such as 'containing', 'transporting' or 'connecting' – is much more valuable than we may appreciate. Schemes are a necessity for all learning, including understanding words and making sense of metaphors (Lakoff & Johnson, 1999). A young child's first recollection of an object, such as a bowl, is not dependent on their figurative recognition of what the object looked like – what Piaget termed a 'schema' – but rather on their operational experience: in other words, what they discover they can do with the bowl (its affordance – what Piaget termed a 'scheme').

Through a child's actions of filling and emptying the bowl (applying their 'containing' scheme), it becomes something understood as a 'container'. The implication is that every 'golden nugget' of knowledge must be understood as having two parts: one figurative (the schema) and the other operative (the scheme).

Neuroscientists have now confirmed this duality in their identification of 'mirror neurons', providing an even stronger empirical basis for what has become commonly known as 'embodied cognition' (Lakoff & Johnson 1999).

Every day, when we come across something new, we try to make sense of it by thinking of what its use might be (ie, what its operational affordance could be). Does it contain something? Could it be used to transport something or to transfer something?

It is through our operational schemes that we are able to make sense of the objects around us.

Another way to see how knowledge is dependent on both scheme and schema is to consider how children learn about animals. To help a child to distinguish between a cat and a dog early on, we may imitate the noises that these animals make, mimic their movements or discuss what they eat. The operations or behaviours of the animals, such as their sounds ('miaow' or 'woof'), help us to distinguish between them.

If we ask a child to look at an object or a picture and we simply offer them the name or the label, the child does not gain a real understanding of what the object is. Hans Furth (1969: 11) neatly explains the problem with rote learning: 'A word is only as good as the knowing structure which uses it.' The figurative word, the image and even the object itself are useless without knowledge of what the object does or can be used for, or how it behaves. Without this operational affordance, we do not understand what it is and therefore the word is meaningless.

From a practical perspective, when a child is exploring a particular scheme, such as the containing/enclosing scheme, we should not only introduce new objects into their play for them to use, enabling them to develop a repertoire of knowledge about different containers (eg, pots, pans, bowls and cups), but also introduce their name(s): 'Jenny, would you like a pan to cook the peas in?'

A story such as Goldilocks and the Three Bears not only supports further exploration of the containing scheme (the exploration of the inside, outside and the barrier between the two), as Jenny fills the bowls with 'porridge' during the storytelling; it also supports her engagement in the story, possibly introducing new vocabulary and an emerging joy of stories.

Children can also be supported in developing new language through the application of a scheme when dancing. For example, a child who enjoys applying a trajectory scheme may enjoy a dance routine which encourages vertical and horizontal trajectory movements: 'Reach up'; 'Roll down'; 'Jump up'; 'Slide to the left' etc. The words are verbalised as each action is performed.

When children apply an operational scheme, they demonstrate what they like to do. If we watch children's play with a keen and knowledgeable eye, we should be able to take a cue from the child as to what they are trying to find out about. It can therefore be said that in their earliest years, children's schemes are a method of communication: 'Look at what I am doing. Help me to delve deeper.' The critical role of the practitioner is to respond to these communications.

Summary

We can see how the environment impacts on communication and wellbeing.

It is really important to understand how the child is exploring their learning environment and what their pattern of play tells us about how they learn and express themselves.

Creating communication-rich environments requires us to be present, mindful and responsive. A flexible approach to the learning environment is essential; as is an understanding that how adults interact and present themselves has a significant influence on how the environment feels for everyone.

Further reading and research ideas

Badger Wood Adventures – Forest School
www.badgerwoodadventures.co.uk

Effective Early Learning and Baby Effective Early Learning
www.crec.squarespace.com/eel-beel

Gemma Goldenberg – Instagram
www.instagram.com/phd_and_three/reels/

Lynnette Brock at Schemaplay
www.schemaplay.com

Make it Wild
www.makeitwild.co.uk

Mandy Johnson at the Soul School for Wellbeing
www.soulschoolforwellbeing.co.uk

Tina Bruce (1991). *Time to Play in Early Childhood Education*. Hodder & Stoughton.

5 | Sharing the love

What is the concept of 'professional love' and what does this look like in the early years environment?

Knowing who we are, both professionally and personally, can help us in exploring how children see the world, what influence this has on practice, and how we react or respond to the emotional context of our role (Richards & Malomo 2022). Rosie Walker (2022) emphasises the importance of supporting educators, and the need for them to recognise who can help them in their role and how to reach out to these people. Understanding ourselves relates deeply to how we professionally love, care for and educate others; how we view the world; and how we perceive childhood and children.

Quite simply, we really do need to know what we believe about loving children; and we need to encompass and support their emotions in a genuine and authentic way. As educators, answering these questions can help us in creating environments of professional love:

DOI: 10.4324/9781003335429-6

- What are your own codes of practice?
- Where will you draw the line for care and education?
- Do you advocate for children and are you heard when you do?
- What culture are you working in and what are the power dynamics?
- Why did you choose to be an educator?
- How do you feel in your role as an educator?
- What do you believe the children are learning with you?
- Is emotional wellbeing for the child and yourself at the heart of your practice?

MINDFUL MOMENT...

Let's reflect on how you feel about love in the educational environment, and how you and your team enable quality interactions that really show the children that they matter. Thoughts and discussions at a team meeting can help sow the seeds of reflective practice, which in turn can create environments of sustained shared thinking.

Thinking about our educational practice is an everyday matter. Take five minutes every day to assess how you taught today and what your sessions felt like to the adults and the children:

- What quality interactions and connections did you create, and how did these make the children feel?
- How does creating connections with the children make you feel?

By reflecting daily on our professional practice, we are building the foundations of our ethos and enhancing our professionalism and in-depth understanding of our practice. Remember, we are never at a standstill. As educators, we continue to learn and develop our own thoughts and brain connections. There will be some children who we find we need to learn more about; our role here is to discover what they are telling us and how best we can help them to thrive. We can only do this when we challenge our own ideas and realise that we can't be right all the time: it is much better to be kind teachers and discover the way forward together.

AN EDUCATOR'S EXPERIENCE...

Let's consider how this might appear in practice by looking at a pro-fessional's efforts to create environments of professional love:

As a childminder, the main thought behind my practice was the level of emotional attachment that I created with each child and family. I invested my time in the child so that they felt safe and secure. You can't do that without having an attachment to the child. With every family I worked with, I ensured that I formed a non-judgemental relationship with them; that our values were aligned; that we all wanted the same for the child. I set out my ethos and discussed this with parents before their child joined my setting. I listened to what they wanted for their child, and we made sure that our ideas were attuned.

Their parents trust you; they need to know you really care.
                                                              Pickering 2023

This educational environment is steeped in care and love. Time for the child is of paramount importance and non-judgemental relationships with families are at the heart of practice. Discussing parents' ideas for and about their child is crucial. By including parents and families in discussions about the child's learning, we are working with them as a team, instead of simply telling them what we know. Honest and open dialogue with families can enable fuller and richer relationships with the child and the key adults in their lives (of whom you are one).

MINDFUL MOMENT...

It is worth you and your team exploring the following thoughts and ideas at the end of the session, once the child has gone home:

* Do you know what sort of day they had?
* What was their deepest engagement in play and who did they connect with?
* Did they tell you anything about their home life and outside world?
* Is this something you can build on and how will they know that you are 'keeping them in mind'?

This short five-minute exercise can really help us to understand the children we work with and enable them to thrive.

When the children are returning home to their families, this is one of the few times that you can build face-to-face, loving, connective relationships with their parents. You can discover more about the child and their life. Handing over the child and explaining what sort of day they have had demonstrates to the family how invested you are in them; how important they are to you; and that you know them well and love them, and enjoy your experiences with them. If you asked most families what they want for their child, their response would probably be that they want them to be happy, now and in the future. How do you create that happiness and joy in your environment?

A great way to develop communication and connections for emotional wellbeing, both for children and for their families, is to ask them what they see as important in the child's lives – communicate! This seems simple to do – and actually, it is! You can start with a quick online Q&A prompt; or you could create your own sheet that you incorporate into children's learning journeys. It is important to remember that we all have different skills and preferences for communication, so we should allow families to communicate with us in the way in which they are most comfortable.

You can build on the information and discussions you have and take this much further in practice. The information that you collate with the team provides vital insight into the child and their life: use it to create an environment that will enable them to thrive and provide enriching experiences for them. By continually listening and developing ways to build trust with families and their children, their voices and ideas become integral to the setting. Ensuring that their voices are heard and understood in different ways demonstrates that they are very important to you, and that they are in partnership with you. The child is seen as the expert on their life (Moss and Clark 2011), and understanding what is important to them helps both the child and the family to see that we believe in them, and will advocate for and with them.

MINDFUL MOMENT...

What do you think of the following reflections – how do they sit with you and your practice?

- Children are one of the biggest treasures that life can bring.
- My eyes light up when the children come into the room.
- We are going to have fun today – every day is different.

- I feel I know each of the children individually.
- I can tell straight away if a child is not feeling connected.
- I know how to support children who are dysregulated.
- There is no such thing as 'naughty'.
- I know I am teaching with emotional intelligence.
- I believe that the children in my setting feel loved.
- I know what is happening to the child's brain when I communicate with them.
- My words and tone are important to how children perceive me.
- Play is crucial for brain development.
- Children come to me with ideas, and I am very happy to support and extend these.
- I trust children and can follow their lead.
- At the end of the session, I evaluate and reflect on how it felt for the children and adults.
- I am an advocate for children and value their knowledge.
- I know when I need to stop and take a break.
- I am aware of how I feel and the influence this has on others.
- My body language and gestures are easily understood by the children and my colleagues.

Dr Jools Page (2018) clarifies Gratzke's belief that love is 'situated' in an early years setting: it is situated in the complex lives, experiences, attitudes, feelings and histories of everyone who participates in the setting. This is a great thought to share with your colleagues.

Developing your curriculum as an educator can be enhanced by taking the time to think. Take another look at the statements above, as these can help to enhance your pedagogical confidence: how you approach your teaching and how you present your curriculum. We always advocate for kinder education and a loving pedagogy. As we know, the foundation of our practice is for children to thrive and develop a love of lifelong learning. We achieve this as educators through the environments of connection and wellbeing that we strive to create every day. We want every child to know that they matter; that they are listened to and are heard.

Further research on the child's voice that could help in developing connections and communications in practice and with children includes *Listening to Young Children – The Mosaic Approach* by Alison Clark and Peter Moss; and *The Voice of the Child: How to Listen Effectively to Young Children* by Julia Maria Gouldsboro.

AN EDUCATOR'S EXPERIENCE...

Here one educator reflects on what professional love feels like in practice:

I have recently returned to early years after a break of 10 years and having my own children, so I am still learning and researching about the best positive practice. I was having a conversation with some children in pre-school and one said 'Ooh, I love you.' I instantly responded with, 'Ooh, I love you too.' Then a few other children said it as well, and we all had a loving moment and a big cuddle.

It was only after that I had a think about that moment and wondered whether it was actually the right thing for me to say, 'I love you too' back to the children. It came naturally to me to want to give the children that love and warmth. I also thought about how it might feel for them if I didn't say it back. I felt that would be awful for them not to have that positive response. So, I instantly

> *responded with professional love for them; and I feel that is the best positive practice to help the children to feel loved and safe with me.*

- How do we build a culture of emotional intelligence and professional love?
- What do the children need to see and hear to feel loved?
- What would you decide to do in this moment when a child tells you they love you?
- How does the word 'love' make you feel?
- What does professional love look like for the children?
- Is love part of our professional role?
- Children need to know they are safe and know that they matter (Knost 2013) – when children feel this, they can play and develop without their energy being diverted to keeping safe in their environment. Do you think the children in this educator's experience are ready to thrive and learn?

Education, it's not about just learning to survive,
*   it's about teaching children to have a life where they understand themselves enough to thrive!*

Poulter Jewson & Skinner 2023

Does professional love matter and who does it matter to?

MINDFUL MOMENT...

- What are your feelings about loving the children who you educate and care for?
- What do you believe professional love should look and feel like for you and for the children you work with?
- What is the ethos of your setting towards loving children and how is this embedded?
- What do children need to thrive and learn?

Let's explore the 'key person' system, where the 'child is kept in mind'. How do we understand this? What does it mean for the child and the educator?

The Early Years Foundation Stage (2021) defines this as follows:

Key person 3.27. Each child must be assigned a key person. Their role is to help ensure that every child's care is tailored to meet their individual needs (in accordance with paragraph 1.16), to help the child become familiar with the setting, offer a settled relationship for the child and build a relationship with their parents.

This relationship is key for children and families, with Page (2018) observing that parents want practitioners to love their children.

What does this really mean for educators in practice? Does this reflect what happens in your setting? Do families understand the importance of your role as a key person; and do they know who is their key person?

Let's unpick this a little further. We are helping the child to settle at their pace and with their own attachment

style; we are valuing what life is like for them; and we are listening to what they are telling us, however they communicate this to us. Relationships, connections and communications are what matter here, and they need to be genuine and thoughtful. We have all been in relationships that, for whatever reason, don't seem to work; and the feeling of being in this situation can be unpleasant and unsettling. We want the best outcomes for the children we work with. Creating robust and secure relationships is a key part of our role; as is valuing, supporting and building the child's emotional intelligence and self-worth.

As a key person, you are also responsible for signposting and engaging specialist help for the child's needs. Ensuring that you really know the children in your care is thus crucial in helping to gain a greater understanding of them. When signposting to other professionals, we need family permission and this can sometimes be a tricky conversation to have with families. Having a trusting relationship with the family, talking with them daily to build communications and connections, asking them their thoughts and valuing these will all help you to obtain the best support for the child.

As a key person, ensure that you ask your line manager or a professional you work with for support when you need it. As a childminder, nanny or lone worker, there are times when you will need support, and having networks of other professionals to discuss and debate with can be helpful and supportive. Many local authorities have an early years adviser whom you can speak with and ask for help.

MINDFUL MOMENT...

You can complete this exercise by yourself and bring it to your next supervision. You might like to think about this in a team meeting. We would always suggest having your own reflective practice file. It often helps to see your journey visually: you can look back and discover more about yourself. This is your safe space to think and question.

Remember, this is your practice and you can challenge your ideas. This is not always easy, but we do need to understand ourselves. This can help us to create thriving lives – not only for ourselves and for our colleagues, but for everyone we connect with. It seems a big responsibility; and indeed it is. Education is like no other career: you hold your own and the children's futures in your mind and in your responses every day.

The headings and thoughts presented below for your reflective practice file are here to help. The more you use reflection in your practice, the easier it becomes to understand and develop it. You are most welcome to change them; to create your own thoughts and ideas that work for you. After all, this is your professional journey, wherever you may be on your early years path.

You can circle a comment or as many as you feel relevant; and you can add your own thoughts. We know that in early years it can get fairly busy, but try to get into the habit of taking five minutes a day to think and reflect.

Educator's reflective practice file – Poulter Jewson and Skinner (2023)

Date and day   *Reflecting on something that didn't go well*

What happened?

It was horrible – It was annoying – It was sad – It was overwhelming – I didn't know what to do

What would I do differently next time?

Nothing – Speak up – Ask for support – Listen – Ask for a moment out

Can I see a pattern in my responses and actions?

Sometimes – Yes – I think I can – Not today – Ah, I did it again – I have felt like this a lot

What are my expectations of myself today?

Low – I am on a high – I'm not really sure – I need to think about this more

How did it make me feel?

Like I wanted to respond – Angry – Upset – Frustrated – Reflective – Not listened to

Why did I feel like that?

I really don't know at the moment – I wanted it to get it right – I had invested a lot of my time –

I thought everyone understood – I didn't know what to do – I needed to take more time – Expectations were too low/high – Responses felt unfair

Do I need to take further action? Do I need to think about this a little bit longer?

Now – Today – Tomorrow – No further action needed

Educator's reflective practice file – Poulter Jewson and Skinner (2023)

Date and day   *Reflecting on something that went well*

What happened?

It felt amazing – This made my day – I kept with it and it worked – I persevered even though this was difficult – I tried a different approach – I responded – The atmosphere was great – Everyone was included – That was easier than I thought

Do I need to change anything?

No, not really – A little tweak – Yes, I do – I'll think about that

Was there a pattern in my responses and actions that I would repeat?

Yes, what I did really worked – I can't see one yet – I think I need to unpick that a little more

What did my expectations of myself and others feel like today?

Spot on – About right – Perhaps a little high – Maybe a little too low – I communicated well

How did it make me feel?

Really brilliant – A bit taken back – I couldn't believe it – Part of a brilliant thing – Very pleased with myself – Pleased with everyone – My hard work paid off – Ecstatic – A bit overwhelmed

Why did I feel like that?

I don't know – Everything just worked well – I got the outcome I wanted – The process has started to happen – I used my voice – I was heard and valued – I connected and responded well – I just didn't expect to feel like this

Do I need to take further action? Do I need to think about this a little bit longer?

Yes I need to keep up this momentum – I need to give this time to settle and embed – I should share this with my colleagues – I am going to reflect on this and sit with it for a while – I am going to take my time and repeat this practice or moment again – I am going to continue to create this positive environment – I will keep listening

---

Everything is difficult before it is easy.

Goethe, Goodreads

It is worth remembering that supervisions are statutory and very necessary. They are also extremely helpful in practice. The idea here is that you talk with your line manager or mentor, often at set periods throughout the year, and cover the aspects of your role that you do not usually have time to sit down and discuss during the everyday routine. You plan and continue your professional journey within this conversation. Your supervisions are written down: both professionals can take notes and any actions are timely and discussed. Seeing ourselves as professionals with a valid purpose and worthy of taking the time for regular discussions enables us to focus and consolidate our ideas and practice (Reed and Walker, 2020).

In an early years setting, if the key person should be the child's 'attachment figure', as policy dictates, it is reasonable to expect that the key person will become invested in the child and, over time, will form a loving, relational bond with the child (Page 2018).

By forming and crafting these natural relationships, and thinking about the child when they are not with you, you show that you are keeping the child in mind. Communicating this to them and sharing their interest can build genuine rapport between the key person and the child. For example, if the child engages deeply with the water tap, the next session you could bring in a pipe or hose for them to extend their play. This demonstrates and communicates to them that they matter to you; that what they think is important to you; that their play is recognised and valued by you. Think about how it feels when we know someone has really thought about us and com-  municated this to us. It doesn't have to be a big gesture – just something that helps the child to know that they matter and that you care. Equally, don't be offended if they don't want to play with the provocation you have brought in – the thought was there and they still know that you were thinking of them.

Emotional coaching responses enable us to support children in a calming manner, with the thought and emphasis being on what is happening for the child right at that moment. How can we support the child's emotions and lessen their anxiety? Tasmin Grimmer (2021) describes the importance of considering the hit of cortisol that the child is experiencing that leads to freeze, flight or fight mode. We, as the educators should offer a calming way out for the child.

Ensuring that we are empathic educators throughout our practice helps each child to feel loved and understood. As educators, we can choose to put ourselves in the child's shoes and understand how it might feel for them when they are upset, angry or non-responsive. We can relate to the child and understand that what we, as adults, may consider to be a little problem is a huge problem for the child and is overwhelming for them. They are not thinking at these moments because they are physically and emotionally unable to do so; their body and brain have become engulfed by anxiety and concern. So, what do we need to do as a consistent adult in their life? We can validate the child's emotions; see what help they might need; be kind, understanding and loving. We can choose to take the kinder education route, which values the child's educational journey as holistic and unique to them. We can support by being an emotionally responsive educator (Dean, Skinner Poulter Jewson and Pickering) who professionally loves and teaches the child through their interests, and who they feel privileged to share their environment with.

AN EDUCATOR'S EXPERIENCE...

An experienced and qualified childminder discusses what professional kindness and love look like in everyday practice:

I love to take the children out and about: we often visit toddler groups where the children can mix and socialise with other children. In my home-based setting, the children always help to make snacks and pour their own drinks. It is a bit different when we stop for juice and biscuits at the toddler group; it is busy and there are often a few spillages. When this happens in my setting, we all help to clear it up and we try to understand that sometimes it doesn't feel nice to get wet – and it can even be a bit of a shock. We can get new clothes (if needed or wanted), and then try again.

One of the little boys I work with doesn't like being even a little wet and will want to get changed straight away. We are working together to show him that it is just a little bit of water or milk; however, at the moment it is too much for him and I respect this. I help him to get changed and we dry his clothes; I show him how quickly they dry and tell him that if he wants to put them back on, he is very welcome to.

This is a calm process, and I feel it is an educational process too. By 'educational', I mean that it is not rushed and we all learn from it. We validate emotions by understanding that it is disappointing when our milk gets spilled; that this does happen, but no one means it to. I always support the child who has spilled the drink and the child it might have spilt on; both can be upset or angry. By staying calm and chatting with them, they gain a new understanding that things like this do happen, and we can cope with them.

At the toddler group, it is a bit different. When there is a spillage, some adults have different ways to deal with this. They don't always help the child or they tell them off for knocking over a drink; the child often becomes more upset and the adult looks cross and fed up. There is a culture of blame, rather than a culture of empathy. I have been trying to model to the children a calm approach and feel that this has the best outcomes for them – and, to be honest, for me as the adult. We can carry on with our day and everyone is happier because we are connected, and the children know my response will be consistent. I always try to think about the fact that the child is learning, and this is part of their everyday emotional development.

Being consistent with children can really help them to feel that they matter.

- Does this feel like professional love in this practice?
- Does it feel like the child's emotions are supported and understood?
- What approach will the children take and how might they treat others when they feel emotionally understood themselves?

- What might the children's future responses be when they spill a drink?
- How connected are the adults' responses to educational outcomes?
- Do the children feel emotionally able to express themselves in a safe space and with a loving and caring professional?
- Which approaches and responses to spilt drinks are more likely to meet the children's emotional needs and build self-esteem?

Further research that could help in practice includes *Developing a Loving Pedagogy in the Early Years* by Tamsin Grimmer (2021) and *Professional Love* by Dr Jools Page (2018).

Sharing information on communication and wellbeing and building partnerships with parents

Why is it important to share information on communication and wellbeing and build partnerships with parents? And how do we do this successfully?

We have unpicked the relationship between communication and emotional wellbeing, and hope that you can see how difficulties with communication skills – be they due to SLCN or the result of a communication breakdown between individuals – can have a major and lifelong impact on emotional wellbeing and on how a child views themselves. This is so important to understand; and while we cannot always resolve or 'fix' communication difficulties, we must create environments in which all children can thrive and are supported in communicating.

We have reflected on our own communications and how, if we get them wrong, our behaviour and actions can result in the child feeling that they are not a good communicator. We must support children in viewing themselves as active communication partners, but we can only do this effectively if we are 'connection creators'.

Parents and carers are typically experts on their own children. They know their children better than anyone else and we must respect this. Through discussion with parents and carers, we can gain insight into how a child's communication difficulties are impacting on their wellbeing; but it is also important to explore how these difficulties may be impacting on the whole family.

Look back to Chapter 3, where we shared personal stories from parents on their experiences of having a child with communication difficulties. The case studies showed parents who are very aware of the impact of communication difficulties on emotional wellbeing and what this means for the whole family. But what is our role when we are working with parents who don't fully understand their child's communication difficulties and how these may be affecting the child's emotional wellbeing?

It can be frustrating and disheartening for families when they are unable to communicate effectively with their child. Parents have fed back to us that they often feel guilty for experiencing these feelings; but these feelings must be acknowledged and validated, just as we would acknowledge and validate the emotions that the child is experiencing when they are unable to communicate their wants and needs effectively. Being available to listen and offer support to parents is essential if we are to develop successful partnerships with them. Listen without judgement and don't try to 'fix' the situation. You can use language to acknowledge what the parent is feeling and listen without judgement – 'You sound frustrated'; 'You seem really sad'; 'You sound angry about that.'

We should help parents to understand the nature of their child's communication difficulties – ideally with the support of a speech and language therapist – and we must respectfully challenge the notion that a child is being lazy with their communication. We have heard this from both parents and practitioners! Children need our understanding and compassion, and having SLCN is not a 'choice'.

Let us also consider how we communicate with parents. The theme throughout this book is that communication is essential in developing successful relationships; and conversely, when communication breaks down, the impact for all those involved is significant. To fully understand a child, we must understand their family and home dynamics, and the part that the child plays in their home situation. Who do they enjoy spending time with? What do they do to keep themselves busy and what motivates and drives them? When we ask these questions, we are starting to 'know' the child and are building a more holistic view of who they are.

Conversations with parents must be balanced and equal. This is especially true for parents of children with additional needs, who may find themselves becoming disempowered as parents. If a whole range of professionals are involved in supporting the child, all offering different suggestions and targets, there is a risk that parents may be overwhelmed and feel that they are unable to speak up about decisions directly related to their child's needs.

We explored the voice of the child and how we can work to ensure that this is heard and respected in detail in Chapter 3. However, we need to go one step further and ensure that the voice of the child is heard whenever we are contributing to decisions around their needs.

MINDFUL MOMENT...

Think about a time when you had a professional conversation about a child. Consider the conversation and how the team decided on the targets and outcomes to set. Did these reflect the child and what is important to them?

We will only be able to discuss this if we have been able to observe and hear the voice of the child and know what matters to them.

Looking after ourselves: why does this matter and how do we do this?

We have already talked about supervisions and we cannot emphasise their importance enough. They are not a time for lots of actions to be put in place or weeks of niggles or questions to be aired; instead, this should happen through discussion within your daily environment, where you should be able to ask questions and evaluate issues together as they arise. Talking honestly every day with your colleagues can help to prevent little things from escalating into big things.

We all have different opinions and views, and we can't expect to agree on everything (Rodd 2013). But we do all need to agree that, as professionals who work with children, we should look after our own wellbeing and feel supported in our role. This is why supervisions are so useful: they give you the opportunity to thrive and discuss what you need; and they give your supervisor the opportunity to support you in moving forward. You should come away from a supervision knowing what you can reflect upon and work on, and what might be next for you in your journey.

Supervisors who listen and can help steer you in the right direction for your career will be good at helping you to seek out more information for your personal and career progression. Supervisors don't do the thinking for you or sort everything out; they listen, signpost and help your ideas come to fruition. You are very much in the driving seat – this is your personal and professional road to travel (Reed & Walker 2020).

MINDFUL MOMENT...

Are educators caught up in a self-perpetuating workload?

We are asking you to be brave and very honest here. Think about your workload and what it feels like to have a work-life balance. You might think that you don't have a balance, and that you often feel you must react and firefight, rather than having time to respond and think. That's okay: you're in the right place; we've got you. Now is the time to take a moment for yourself, breathe and have a cuppa. You could perhaps get a pen and paper and write down your thoughts. Have a think about what small change could you make today: what would really help you to be you and to change your workload patterns? How can you take the time for what you need? These small reflective changes can help in establishing a better work-life balance.

We love inspirational quotes: they say in a 'nutshell' what we are trying to explain. We suggest printing out and putting up your favourite thoughts, to remind you how significant you are to your own life.

We can think of self-care as a bit like the roots of a tree: they start off little and grow; they become anchored and grounded; shoots get bigger and more robust; with time and care, they develop and grow into a magnificent tree. Everything takes time to cultivate; however, being aware of the time we need to grow and ensuring we take at least a moment every day can help us all to thrive.

Remember the branches of a tree can bend, however with too much pressure they can also break, we can all be flexible, but we cannot control the storm.

Poulter 2020

Self-care is not a quick fix when we are feeling exhausted; it should be done every day for you to be you. Talk to someone who will listen; reflect; write down your thoughts and try to unravel your patterns of emotional behaviour and communication style where possible. Speak to a professional therapist when you need to – they are experts at helping people. Leaving things as they are, when you are exhausted or unhappy, will not usually help you to feel any better. It's okay to sit with things for a while; however, make sure you are your priority. Being in a career you love and enjoy should enhance your enjoyment of life. There can be a few obstacles, but we can overcome these and continue to develop professionally and personally.

MINDFUL MOMENT...

Here are a few questions that could be considered either honest or contentious – but whichever way you envisage them, they do need to be voiced, heard and reflected upon so that we can carry out our role as educators to the best of our ability and enable children and family's emotional wellbeing and communications to thrive:

- As educators, are we unintentionally conserving and prolonging the problem of overworking?
- What do we think about the statement 'If I don't do it, no one else will'?
- Is there an educational environmental mindset of, 'We all do extra no matter what the cost to us'?
- Educators' intentions are honourable and come from a desire to help and change lives. Are we doing more than we can to do good and help others at the expense of our own emotional wellbeing?
- Can you say a polite 'No thank you' to extra tasks when you feel overwhelmed?

Being in a supportive culture where work is carried out on time can feel great. This does not mean it's not a busy environment or that there are no deadlines; it means that people are seen, heard and valued. Having a good time at work and creating a culture of enjoyment helps professionals to be more productive.

MINDFUL MOMENT...

Here's one more saying we would love you to keep in mind: *you cannot pour from an empty cup.* You need time to top up – and the more frequently, the better (Cater 2021). Have a think what this means for you and how you can start to top up daily. Two minutes is better than no minutes.

- Educators can often be asked to work overtime to attend team meetings until late, which can often mean an 11 or 12-hour shift. How do you feel if you do this?
- What does your practice feel like when you are tired? Do you feel that your role is sustainable at this pace?
- As an educator, do you agree to take on extra responsibilities when you know this will overwhelm you?
- Should educators take work home and work extra hours even if they know that this will have a detrimental effect on their work-life balance?

Know when to say no; when to rest; when to stop

Being in a profession where kindness to others comes as the norm means that we also need to be kind to ourselves. Remember, we need to **know** when to say **no**, when to **rest** and when to **stop**. This is an act of kindness to ourselves, and to the families and children we work with. We care and empathise in this amazing career we have chosen; but this does not mean that we must place our own needs last. There will always be other people joining our career and one of our key roles as educators is to model to them how to look after their own emotional wellbeing and place this and the children at the heart of their practice, sharing the power of communication and connection.

Saying a polite no before you are nearing your limit is an act of kindness to yourself, and a skill that we all need to master.

Poulter Jewson & Skinner 2022

How can we raise the profile of what we do and how important the early years are?

Understanding our crucial role in our early years career can help educators to value their place in their community and in building society.

We do need to mention funding for early years – this is vital in ensuring that professionals' and families' finances are considered fairly. Considering the role that you fulfil in early years, the remuneration should be much higher. Know your professional worth; try not to perpetuate the cycle of, 'There  is no money in early years – we do it for the love of it.' Yes, we do love our role as educators; however, we are professionals with a lot of responsibility, experience and skills, and with generations of children and families depending upon us.

The remuneration of early-years professionals is not commensurate with the skills and responsibility involved. Funding for early years educators will need to level up and reflect the duty, care and education that we provide. Channel your passion and pride in your profession to speak up and advocate for early years professionals. We should seek to change the norm and be part of the discussion.

We often hear, 'It's just play,' or 'I'm just the key person.' Let's change this and start to say, 'It's all about play,' and highlight the importance of this for brain development and for building environments in which children's communications are really listened to and valued.

Let's continue positive communications, such as, 'I am an early years educator and I know the positive difference I can help to make for children and families now and for their futures.' Oh yes: we help to build the foundations of future society through understanding play. We need you to believe that your communications will and do count. You need to promote and support your career choice vociferously. Is early years education one of the best careers in the world? We think so! You are helping to shape future lives and leaders. Tread mindfully and value children now: they will one day decide your future, your community and your social order.

We must always think of our role as brain scientists, brain shapers, brain researchers. We are not just saying this; it is what educators do. If you don't talk, don't interact, aren't kind and don't show children that they matter, their brains will physically build connections in a different way, their self-worth will be lower and they may not thrive.

Advice for educators

At school, childcare is not always viewed as an 'academic' career, so some people may choose it as it is considered more hands-on and practical. Others may pursue it on the basis that they are good with children. But whether you left school with fewer qualifications or have fallen into the role of an educator by becoming a parent or volunteering, this is where your lifelong education can continue. This is where you become a researcher, by trying to understand what makes a child 'tick' and how they communicate with you.

Every person has their own strengths and ideas. When people feel that their ideas are being listened to and heard, they start to believe in themselves. There are apprenticeships and opportunities to gain qualifications where you work; and you could go on to college or university when you are ready, there are many flexible courses available. Early years education requires the best of you: you have to be 'on top form' every day. Choose wisely where you work; look out for mentors; ask about help to study; observe the kindness in the environment you choose.

Surround yourself with advocates for children who enable them to flourish and will support them when needed. Always voice your thoughts and reflect on the fact that we can't always be right about everything, but we can always be kind. Understand and excel at your role in education: you can and you will make a difference in the world, one child at a time. Your role is one of the most important positions and a career in education is a dynamic one. You are working with young children, and they need you to be a brilliant activist, to innovate and advocate for them.

Early years leads (including childcare leads, managers and owners)

Step out of the office; spend time with the children, families and the team. If you feel like you are in an administrative role, it may be better to employ an admin assistant so that you can dedicate your expertise to the children and carry out only child-related essential office work.

Reflect on your communication and leadership style. You have a vital responsibility in your role: society looks to you to create environments that will shape lives. Set and adhere to an ethos where you cherish and educate children, and always demonstrate kinder education. Build those brains with the children, their families and your team. Support and nurture every educator; help them to build their career paths, even if this means that they move on and choose a different role.

By being proactive, you can positively enhance wider communities of children and their education. The individuals and teams that you work with are meant to grow and develop. They are integral to change, and can advocate widely for children's play, emotional wellbeing and communication. Lead well; ask for support when you need it; distribute your leadership; and trust others. Helping people to believe in themselves and develop their understanding is a crucial and rewarding part of being a leader. Being a leader does not mean we are supposed to have all the best ideas or get everything right – no one can. To make decisions as leaders we reflect, respond, and listen. How we communicate our thoughts and ideas is integral to the professional environments we create.

The Beckies

Expand your horizons

Being part of a wider community can really help. There are bodies and campaigns that are highlighting the importance of early years. Use your professional voice; communicate and join in with your thoughts. You have chosen a wonderful profession – please be very proud of yourself for your dedication and commitment to enhancing young children's lives. Get involved: your opinion, reflections and expertise matter.

Early years educators = brain scientists

Connect with this awesome community of early years advocates:

- Thriving Language CIC
- Thriving Language Podcasts
- The Royal Foundation Centre for Early Childhood
- Early Years Alliance
- Early Years Education
- EYTV – Kathy Brodie
- Liz Pemberton – The Black Nursery Manager
- Dr Mine Conkbayir
- SchemaPlay CIC
- Badger Wood Adventures
- #ShapingUs
- #WeAreEducators
- #Brainscientists
- #quailtyinteractions
- #thrivingey
- #developmentmatters

Summary

When you work with children, you are in a privileged position! The moment you walk through the door or the moment the first children arrive at your setting, you must view yourself as an educator. No matter what your level of qualification, you are always teaching in your role. You are teaching when you greet the children; you are teaching when you support washing hands, or putting shoes and coats on. Our biggest responsibility in teaching in the early years is to respect and value the children's play, and to do that we need to understand what the play means for each individual child.

We must all value our role in understanding and teaching children, and we must work together to raise the profile of this incredible profession.

As you reach the end of this book, take a moment to think: what are you going to do with this information, and how are you going to advocate for your career and the children you work with?

Further reading and research ideas

Alison Clark and Peter Moss (2017). *Listening to Young Children, A Guide to Understanding and Using the Mosaic Approach*, expanded third edition. National Children's Bureau.

Julia Maria Gouldsboro (2017). *The Voice of the Child: How to Listen Effectively to Young Children*. Routledge

Dr Jools Page and Cathy Nutbrown (2013). *Working with Babies and Children: From Birth to Three*. Sage.

Kate Moxley (2022). *A Guide to Mental Health for Early Years Educators – Putting Wellbeing at the Heart of Your Philosophy and Practice*. Routledge.

Michael Reed and Rosie Walker (2020). 'The importance and value of mentoring and coaching in the early years.' In Michael Gasper and Rosie Walker (eds) *Coaching and Mentoring in Early Childhood*. Bloomsbury.

References

Atkinson, M. and McHanwell, S. (2002). *Basic Medical Science for Speech and Language Therapy Students.* Wiley.

Benoit, D. (2004). 'Infant-parent attachment: Definition, types, antecedents, measurement and outcome.' *Paediatric Child Health,* 9 (8): 541–545.

Brock, L. (2022). *Schemaplay: Improving Learning Outcomes For All Children Through Free-Flow Play.* https://schemaplay.com/author/lybrock/ (accessed January 2023).

Brock, L. and Siraj-Blatchford, J. (2019). *SchemaPlay Activity Ideas: Supporting learning outcomes in free-flow play.* SchemaPlay Publications.

Bruce, T. (1991). *Time to Play in Early Childhood Education.* Hodder & Stoughton.

Bryan, K., Freer J. and Furlong C. (2007). 'Language and communication difficulties in juvenile offenders.' *International Journal of Language and Communication Disorders,* 42 (5): 505–520.

Cater, L. (2021). *"You Can't Pour From an Empty Cup": Why Self-Care Isn't Selfish.* https://modern-minds.com/you-cant-pour-from-an-empty-cup-why-self-care-isnt-selfish (accessed February 2023).

Clark, A. and Moss, P. (2011). *Listening To Young Children: The Mosaic Approach* (2nd ed). National Children's Bureau.

Conkbayir, M. (2017). *Early Childhood and Neuroscience: Theory, Research and Implications for Practice.* Bloomsbury.

Conkbayir, M. (2023). *The Neuroscience of the Developing Child: Self-Regulation for Wellbeing and a Sustainable Future.* Routledge.

Csikszentmihalyi, M. (2008). *Flow: The Psychology of Optimal Experience*. Ingram International inc.

Delahooke, M. (2020). *Beyond Behaviours. Using Brain Science and Compassion to Understand and Solve Children's Behavioural Challenges*. John Murray Learning.

Department for Education (2021). *Statutory Framework for the Early Years Foundation Stage: Setting the Standards for Learning, Development and Care for Children from Birth to Five*. https://assets.publishing.service.gov.uk/government/uploads/system/uploads/attachment_data/file/974907/EYFS_framework_-_March_2021.pdf (accessed November 2022).

Early Years Coalition (2021). *Birth to Five Matters: Non-Statutory Guidance for the Early Years Foundation Stage*. Early Education.

Eliot, L. (1999). *What's Going on in There? How the Brain and Mind Develop in the First Five Years*. Bantam Books.

Evans, A.C. (2021). *What is Communication? - Definition & Importance*. https://study.com/academy/lesson/what-is-communication-definition-importance.html (accessed May 2022).

Garrick, R. (2009). *Playing Outdoors in the Early Years* (2nd ed.). Continuum International Publishing Group.

Grimmer, T. (2021). *Developing a Loving Pedagogy in the Early Years: How Love Fits with Professional Practice*. Routledge.

Hollo, A., Wehby, J.H., and Oliver, R.M. (2014). 'Unidentified Language Deficits in Children with Emotional and Behavioral Disorders: A Meta-Analysis.' *Exceptional Children*, 80(2), 169–186.

Knost, L. (2013). *Two Thousand Kisses a Day: Gentle Parenting Through the Ages and Stages*. Little Hearts Books, LLC.

Kurt, S. (2020). *Maslow's Hierarchy Of Needs In Education*. https://educationlibrary.org/maslows-hierarchy-of-needs-in-education/ (accessed September 2022).

Law, J. Peacey, N. and Radford, J. (2020). Department for Education and Employment, corp creator. 'Provision for children with speech and language needs in England and Wales: facilitating communication between education and health services.' [Research report (Great Britain. Department for Education and Employment); No 239.]

Lilley, L. (1967). *Friedrich Froebel. A Selection from His Writings.* Cambridge University Press.

Lindsay, G. and Dockrell, J. (2012). The relationship between speech, language and communication needs (SLCN) and behavioural, emotional and social difficulties (BESD). Department for Education Research Report DFE-RR247-BCRP6.

Malaguzzi, L. (1996). *The Hundred Languages of Children: The Reggio Emilia Approach to Early Childhood Education.* Ablex Publishing Corporation.

Manners, L. (2019). *The Early Years Movement Handbook: A Principles-Based Approach to Supporting Young Children's Physical Development, Health and Wellbeing.* Jessica Kingsley Publishers.

McEwin, A. and Santow, E. (2018). 'The importance of the human right to communication.' *International Journal of Speech-Language Pathology,* 20 (1): 1–2.

Mead, M. (1973). *Margaret Mead: Human Nature and the Power of Culture.* https://www.loc.gov/exhibits/mead/field-sepik.html (accessed September 2022).

Mort, S. (2021). *A Manual for Being Human: What Makes Us Who We Are, Why it Matters and Practical Advice for a Happier Life.* Simon and Schuster UK.

Moxley, K. (2022). *A Guide to Mental Health for Early Years Educators: Putting Wellbeing at the Heart of Your Philosophy and Practice.* Routledge.

Murray, J. (2019). 'Hearing young children's voices.' *International Journal of Early Years Education,* 27 (1): 1–5.

Page, J. (2013). 'Do mothers want professional carers to love their babies?' *Journal of Early Childhood Research,* 9 (3): 310–323.

Page, J. (2018). 'Characterising the principles of Professional Love in early childhood care and education.' *International Journal of Early Years Education,* 26 (2): 125–141.

Perry, B. (2009). 'Examining child maltreatment through a neurodevelopmental lens: clinical applications of the neurosequential model of therapeutics.' *Journal of Loss and Trauma,* 14: 240–255.

Poulter Jewson, R. and Skinner, R. (2022). *Speech and Language in the Early Years: Creating Language-Rich Learning Environments*. Routledge.

Reed, M. and Walker, R. (2020). *The Importance and Value of Mentoring and Coaching in the Early Years*. In Gasper, M. and Walker, R. (eds) *Coaching and Mentoring in Early Childhood*. Bloomsbury.

Rodd, J. (2013). *Leadership in Early Childhood: The Pathway to Professionalism* (4th ed). Open University Press.

Romeo R.R., Segaran J., Leonard J.A., Robinson S.T., West M.R., Mackey A.P., Yendiki A, Rowe M.L. and Gabrieli JDE. (2018). 'Language exposure relates to structural neural connectivity in childhood.' *Journal of Neuroscience*, 38 (36): 7870–7877.

Siegel, D. (2012). *The Developing Mind: How Relationships and the Brain Interact to Shape Who We Are*. Guildford Press.

Solihull Approach (2014). *Solihull Approach Trainers' Manual*. Jill Rogers Associates Ltd. First published 2002.

Stackhouse, J. and Wells, B. (1997). *Children's Speech and Literacy Difficulties: A Psycholinguistic Framework*. Whurr.

Stinnett, T., Reddy, V. and Zabel, M. (2022). 'Neuroanatomy, Broca area.' In: StatPearls [Internet]. StatPearls Publishing.

Torr, J. and Pham, L. (2016). Educator Talk in Long Day Care Nurseries: How Context Shapes Meaning. *Early Childhood Educ J*, 44, 245–254.

Ulset, V., Vitaro, F., Brendgen, M., Bekkhus, M. and Borge, A. (2017). 'Time spent outdoors during preschool: links with children's cognitive and behavioral development.' *Journal of Environmental Psychology*, 52: 69–80.

Walker, R. (2022). Chapter 9, edited by Hazel Richards and Michelle Malomo. *Developing Your Professional Identity: A Guide for Working with Children and Families*. Critical Publishing Ltd.

Watkins, S. (2022). *Outdoor Play for Healthy Little Minds. Practical Ideas to Promote Children's Wellbeing in the Early Years*. Routledge.

Wiking, M. (2016). *The Little Book of Hygge: The Danish Way to Live Well*. Penguin Life.

Zeedyk, S. (2020) *Sabre Tooth Tigers & Teddy Bears: The Connected Baby Guide to Understanding Attachment* (2nd ed). Connected Baby.

Websites

https://www.bbc.co.uk/news/world-asia-64330859 (accessed November 2022).

https://www.cdacanada.com/ (accessed June 2022).

www.earlyyearseducator.co.uk (accessed December 2022).

https://ecdpeace.org/work-content/world-organization-early -childhood-education-omep#:~:text=OMEP%20is%20an %20international%2C%20non,care%20(ECEC)%20since%201948 (accessed September 2022).

https://www.facebook.com/watch/?v=368442640668920 (accessed November 2022).

https://www.froebel.org.uk/ (accessed June 2022).

https://www.health.nsw.gov.au/kidsfamilies/programs/Pages/first-2000 -days (accessed July 2022).

https://www.facebook.com/Kindereducation/ (accessed July 2022).

https://www.montessori.org/ (accessed October 2022).

https://www.ncbi.nlm.nih.gov/books/NBK568743/ (accessed May 2022).

https://www.oed.com/ (accessed October 2022).

https://www.reggiochildren.it/en/reggio-emilia-approach/ (accessed July 2022).

https://www.sciencedirect.com/science/article/abs/pii/ S0272494417300737 (accessed May 2022).

https://www.speechandlanguage.org.uk/talking-point/parents/ages -and-stages/ (accessed May 2022).

https://www.study.com/academy/lesson/what-is-communication -definition-importance.html (accessed May 2022).

https://www.thrivinglanguage.co.uk (accessed June 2022).

https://www.unicef.org/sites/default/files/2018-12/UNICEF-Lego -Foundation-Learning-through-Play.pdf (accessed June 2022).

https://worldhappiness.report/ed/2018/ (accessed November 2022).

https://worldhappiness.report/ed/2022/ (accessed November 2022).

https://worldpopulationreview.com/country-rankings/hdi-by-country (accessed October 2022).

Podcasts

Thriving Language podcast (2022) with Gemma Goldberg: New Research – The impact of environments on children's development, play & learning https://podcasts.apple.com/gb/podcast/new -research-the-impact-of-environments-on/id1512213209?i =1000545272541

Index